WORLD
RALLY
CHAMPIONSHIP
GUIDE 2001

THIS IS A CARLTON BOOK

This edition published in 2001 by
Carlton Books Limited
20 Mortimer Street
London W1T 3JW

10 9 8 7 6 5 4 3 2 1

A CIP catalogue record for this book is available from the British
Library

ISBN 1 84222 190 6

Executive Editor: Chris Hawkes
Project Art Direction: Gavin Tyler
Production: Sarah Corteel
Picture Research: Debora Fioravanti

Printed and bound in Italy

KEITH OSWIN has been involved in rallying for almost
three decades. For two of them he has been a journalist and was
Rallies Editor for the world's leading motorsport magazine,
Autosport. During his tenure of that post he learned about
rallying from the hot seat, co-driving for several of the sport's top
names including Jimmy McRae, Per Eklund and four-time World
Champion, Tommi Makinen. He is one of the few British
journalists to have attended every World Championship event in
recent seasons and is therefore ideally qualified to compile this
fans' guide to the exciting world of rallying.

WORLD
RALLY
CHAMPIONSHIP
GUIDE 2001

Keith Oswin

CARLTON
BOOKS

CONTENTS

FOREWORD BY COLIN McRAE

This book is being launched at the most exciting time that rallying has enjoyed for years. It's all very exciting and the potential is fantastic. It's good that someone has had the balls to grab the opportunity and run with the idea.

Rallying is really very strong at the moment and there are plenty of manufacturers involved. In fact you can tell how strong it is because losing a major manufacturer like SEAT for 2001 hasn't been the body blow that it would have been a few years ago when only two or three teams were competing regularly. We're actually gaining Citroen as a replacement, but the sport would still be strong even if that wasn't the case. There are a lot of changes taking place and that will continue over the next two or three years. So far, all the changes have been for the better.

However, no sport can afford to stand still for long these days. People are putting more and more money into rallying and they want value for that money. What David Richards is doing with the television rights will certainly improve that, so it looks like we're heading in the right direction. He knows what he wants to achieve, although the practicalities may force him to adopt a slightly different plan to the one in his head at the moment.

On the driver front we've seen guys like Petter Solberg and Markko Martin get works drives despite coming from relatively obscure countries. Two years ago you'd never have thought that a Norwegian and an Estonian would be the hottest new talent in rallying, but that's what happened with Petter and Markko. I think that the new junior formulae like the Super 1600 championship will be an important step in giving young drivers a good opportunity to make a name for themselves. It's all new territory but it could spring a few surprises in a year or two's time.

New teams, new drivers and also new events are all part of the changing face of rallying. Cyprus wasn't an especially enjoyable event for a driver because it was so twisty, but it was just one piece of a much larger jigsaw and it would be wrong to criticise it for that. If taking the sport to new countries is a benefit for the championship then I'm in favour of it.

I'm naturally disappointed not to have won the championship last year having been in the hunt so close to the end. Winning would have meant that all the hard work we've put in at Ford over the past two years, and the frustrations of the past few seasons, had paid off. I've been very close to winning the championship several times in the past few years, so going the whole way would be a bit of payback for that as well!

Hopefully, I can put that right this season and come back to write the foreword for the 2002 version of this book as World Champion.

ANALYSIS OF THE 2001 SEASON

If the first World Rally Championship of the 21st century was a classic then the upcoming season could be even better. With six serious manufacturers now firmly established, and Citroen expected to join the gang full time before many more years are up, the titles are becoming ever more hotly contested.

The star names are lined up and ready to go but will it be McRae, Burns, Sainz, Gronholm or Makinen taking the crown in 2001?

Ford finally has got the Focus really flying, Peugeot emerged over the past season as a worthy champion and title favourite again this season while Subaru goes to the start line in Monte Carlo with another new Impreza. While these three can be expected to be the headline-makers, Mitsubishi must find the technical equivalent of Viagra to give its ageing Lancer a much-needed lift to get back to the top. Hopefully, the WRC version will be just that.

Hyundai needs a test budget to capitalise on last year's experience and join the big hitters while Skoda already is edging into the big league.

All in all it's a year you don't want to miss.

FORD

When Ford moved its rally team into a former mental hospital, some wondered if the oldest manufacturer in the pack had gone mad. But Ford is now enjoying a renaissance and, after more than two decades, the good times just might be back at last.

Until Subaru and Colin McRae came along, British rally fans nailed their colours to Ford's mast. Throughout the seventies the Blue Oval reigned supreme in their hearts, even if their head-to-head battles with the Fiat/Lancia empire went the Italians' way more often than not. Anoraks, bobble hats and even the cars they drove to the stages showed that if you cut a British rally fan in half there would be a Ford logo right through the middle.

Underpinning this success was the Ford Escort, introduced in the late 1960s and carrying Ford's name through the following decade, in various evolutions, to success after success. Event wins and championship titles had been going Ford's way long before the World Championship was even dreamed of, let alone created. And then it all went wrong.

The four-wheel drive revolution caught Ford on the hop and the team retreated to try to find a successor to the Escort while the likes of Audi

Frustratingly unreliable, but also astonishingly quick, the Focus has put Ford back on top.

and Peugeot were already up and running with their Group B supercars. By the time Ford got its RS200 challenger ready it was too late and, thanks to the marketing men, too compromised compared with its rally-bred rivals.

Group A offered Ford a lifeline, but the company still produced a series of unsuitable vehicles before it finally got a grip and built its first 'proper' rally car for over a decade – the Escort Cosworth.

Statistics can be made to prove anything, of course, but a look at Ford's winning record shows just how clearly the mighty had fallen. From the first year of the World Championship (in 1973) Ford enjoyed event success every year until 1981. It then endured a seven-year gap before its next win and a further five years before the next. During the 1973–1979 period Ford won 17 World Championship rallies while the 1980s brought only five wins. It was heartbreaking to watch and just as frustrating for those inside the team as one of the most powerful manufacturers in the world struggled even to be considered a serious contender at times.

The return of the Escort name, however, saw an upturn in both fortunes and morale, although it was fast becoming clear that a major change still was needed. A string of motorsport directors had their chance to do something about Ford, but it wasn't until Martin Whitaker (a former journalist and communications manager with an impressive pedigree) joined the company in 1995 that the future started to become clear.

By the end of 1996 he had done the unthinkable and detached Ford's rally team from its three-decade-old residence at Boreham Airfield in Essex and sent it north to Malcolm Wilson's new M-Sport base in Cumbria. Wilson, a former British Champion driver, had long been loyal to Ford despite more than a few kicks in

THE VIPS

MALCOLM WILSON

A former British Rally Champion, Wilson has rarely been separated from the Ford name in 25 years. His M-Sport company was founded to take the Ford team from its spiritual home in 1996.

GUENTHER STEINER

Italian-born engineer Steiner worked with rally teams at Mazda, Lancia and Subaru before joining M-Sport to head the design team for the Ford Focus WRC project in 1998.

the teeth from previous management, and was now handed the responsibility for running the show.

What might have seemed a poisoned chalice turned out to be a golden opportunity for Wilson. He inherited the Escort World Rally Car from Boreham and, thanks to a massive input from star driver Carlos Sainz, began to get results.

What Ford and M-Sport really needed, however, was a no-compromise car of its own, designed from the wheels up to win the modern World Rally Championship. The Escort was killed off once again and in its place came the Focus, designed and built in secret at Millbrook

The buck stops here. Malcolm Wilson is the man in charge.

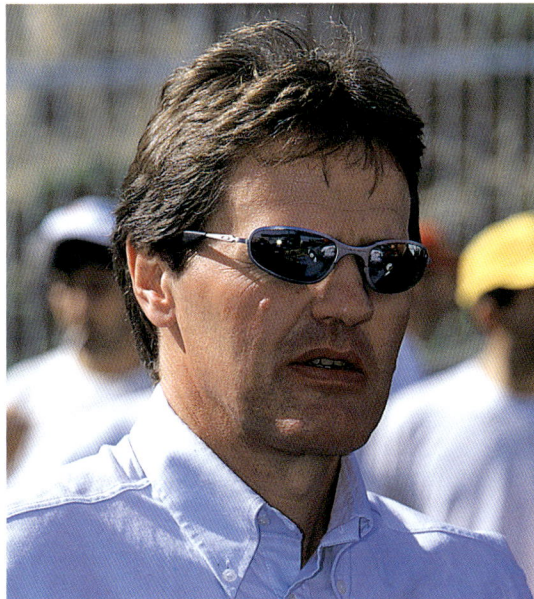

and emerging for the 1999 World Rally Championship.

Sainz had returned to Toyota, but Ford showed just how committed it was to getting back to the winning circle by snatching Colin McRae from Subaru for a staggering $10 million over two years. The size of his salary sent shock waves through the sport, because it brought rallying into the Formula 1 price bracket.

The first season for the Focus was a bitter-sweet affair. There was controversy over its water pump that eventually got it thrown out of the Monte Carlo Rally, joy when it won the Safari and Portugal rallies and despair when reliability deserted it later in the year. However the performance was enough to tempt Sainz back to the camp in 2000 and the fiery partnership of the Scot and the Spaniard was as exciting to watch as it was difficult to control.

Meanwhile Ford opened its multi-million pound motorsport centre at Dovenby Hall on the edge of Cumbria's Lake District. This was once a mental hospital, but this state of the art facility now puts even the great Formula 1 teams to shame.

Without a doubt Ford is back. Winning is never easy in modern World Championship rallying but, for the first time in a long time, Ford goes to the start of each event as a serious contender and no longer a team that's just there to make up the numbers.

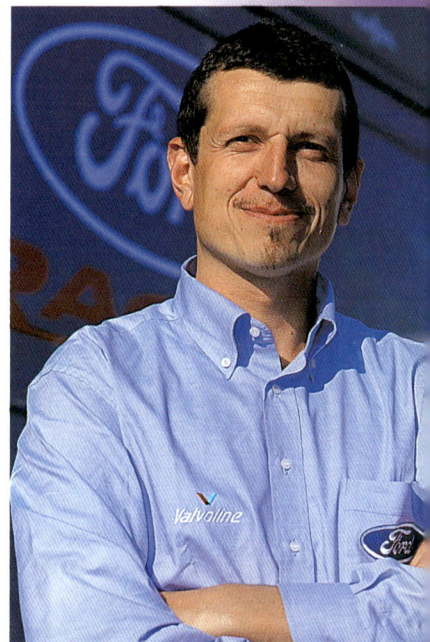

Guenther Steiner is the man who created Ford's WRC rally weapon.

FOR THE RECORD

Country of origin: Britain
Team base: Cockermouth, England
Date of formation: 1996 (M-Sport)
WRC debut: Monte Carlo 1973
First WRC win: 1973 1,000 Lakes
WRC wins: 37
Manufacturers titles: 1979*
Drivers titles: 1979 (Bjorn Waldegard), 1981 (Ari Vatanen)

Team specification

Car: Ford Focus WRC   **Tyres:** Pirelli
Sponsors: Martini, Valvoline, Telefonica MoviStar
Team principal: Malcolm Wilson   **Designer:** Guenther Steiner

COLIN McRae

Colin McRae is one of the most exciting rally drivers ever to grace a special stage. His aggressive driving style has endeared him to rally fans the world over who know that, whenever he pulls on his helmet, they are guaranteed thrill-a-minute action.

Colin McRae is Britain's fastest and most exciting driver for decades.

McRae was born to rally. His dad, Jimmy, was five-time British Champion and his younger brother, Alister, also joined the family 'business'. McRae also changed the face of British rallying and opened the door for the likes of Richard Burns to follow in his footsteps.

The McRae legend began towards the end of the 1980s when Peugeot spotted his talent and signed him for the 1988 'Young Lions' team. He moved on to the world stage with a private Ford Sierra Cosworth, where his habit of mixing blistering speed with spectacular accidents established the 'McCrash' tag.

The turning point came when Subaru boss David Richards had the vision (and the bravery) to sign the young Scot to drive the new Subaru Legacy on a Rothmans-backed British Championship campaign in 1991. McRae won the title that season and, with a whitewash of all six events, retained it the following season. That put both car and driver on the map and McRae stayed at Subaru for eight consecutive seasons.

In McRae's second year at Subaru, he embarked on a limited WRC programme. Rival drivers quickly learned that McRae was a star in the making when he took second on the Swedish Rally and regularly set stage times that made the establishment take notice.

New Zealand 1993 really turned McRae into a star. Not since Roger Clark's 1976 RAC Rally victory had a British driver won a World Championship rally, but McRae blitzed the Kiwi event to end the drought. He took two more New Zealand rallies in succession to make it his own, but already had his sights set on higher things.

Winning the RAC Rally of 1994 added another page to the record books (Clark's 1976 win was also the previous success for a British driver), but it was defeating team-mate Carlos Sainz on the same rally the following year that brought McRae the World title he craved.

Over the next two seasons he stayed loyal to Subaru, but there were occasions when the relationship became frosty and it probably was to everyone's benefit that he took the decision to break with his long-time employer for 1999. Ford's announcement that he was to be paid $10 million over the next two seasons, however, sent shock waves through the sport. McRae's salary showed that Ford was now taking rallying into Formula 1 territory, and underlined the seriousness of the Focus project.

McRae showed a patient side to his nature as the car developed in its first year, although he went close to calling it quits after reliability problems in its second. By the middle of the season, however, McRae and Ford were winning again, and he has signed for at least another two years.

STAGE NOTES

Nationality: Scottish
Born: August 5, 1968, Lanark, Scotland
Teams: Vauxhall 1987, Peugeot 1988, Ford 1989–1990, Subaru 1991–1998, Ford 1999–

Career record

First rally: 1986 with Talbot Avenger
WRC debut: 1987 Swedish (Vauxhall Nova, 36 o/a)
WRC starts: 101 **WRC wins:** 20
1993 New Zealand; 1994 New Zealand, Britain; 1995 New Zealand, Britain; 1996 Acropolis, San Remo, Catalunya; 1997 Safari, Corsica, San Remo, Australia, Britain; 1998 Portugal, Corsica, Acropolis; 1999 Safari, Portugal; 2000 Catalunya, Acropolis
Stage wins: 415
Honours: 1991 & 1992 British Champion, 1995 World Champion, 1996 awarded MBE.

CARLOS SAINZ

Carlos Sainz's claim to fame is as a rally driver, but as a talented all-round sportsman he could have made his name in several other areas. Nevertheless he remains one of rallying's all-time greats and one of the toughest competitors in the business.

At first Sainz couldn't decide whether to go racing or rallying so he tried both. In 1981 he won the SEAT Panda rally championship before adding the Renault 5 race series the following year and, just for good measure, won both the race and rally version of the Renault 5 Turbo series the year after.

He twice finished runner up in the Spanish Championship with Renault (1985 and 1986) before Ford's satellite operation, run by Mike Little in Cumbria, took up the reins and guided him in 1987 to both the national title and a sensational World Championship debut in Portugal. Although he didn't finish, the young upstart stunned the establishment by setting the fastest time on the opening stage. He also took his first WRC points in both that season's Corsica and RAC rallies.

In the following year Sainz (and new co-driver Luis Moya), retained the Spanish title and contested seven World Championship events, never finishing lower than seventh.

Sainz bade an emotional farewell to Ford at the end of the season, because the team had no four-wheel drive car in the planning. That's what he needed to go the next step, so he signed for Toyota in 1989 and stayed there for the next four years. It is hard to say which he would choose but, if Sainz has a spiritual home outside of Spain, then it would be with either Ford or Toyota.

His second year at Cologne put him on the global map. Victories in Greece, New Zealand, Finland (he was the first of only two non-Scandinavian drivers ever to win this event) and Britain clinched his first world title.

Inexplicably he chose to leave Toyota for a semi-works Lancia in 1993 and slumped to eighth in the series after a year where he never looked like winning a thing. From 1990–1998 this was the only year that he finished outside the top three in the championship. At Subaru, where he moved after his Lancia hiatus, he found himself paired with Colin McRae and the pair never really hit it off.

Sainz announced his intention to return to Toyota for 1996 just as Toyota was banned for the season! In a quick reshuffle he returned to Ford and instantly raised the game at the fledgling M-Sport operation. In both 1996 and 1997 he was third in the championship and collected more wins before Toyota tempted him back. He opened his account with victory on the Monte Carlo Rally in 1998, but after two seasons he was back at Ford and, ironically, paired again with McRae. The relationship was still tense but there remains no sign that Sainz is about to give up his quest for success, no matter who stands in his way.

Carlos Sainz is arguably the most competitive driver in the sport today.

HYUNDAI

Hyundai's Accent WRC project took the Korean manufacturer right to the forefront of World Rally and brought up the seventh major team in the rapidly expanding series. Last season was very much a development year for Hyundai and was painful at times.

The Accent WRC has had a difficult start, but has shown plenty of promise.

Of all the leading teams in the World Rally Championship, Hyundai has been around for the fewest number of years. Milton Keynes-based Motor Sport Developments (MSD) took over the running of the team in 1998 with an eye on the 1999 season but, even then, Hyundai had little more than a year's experience.

The team's initial forays into rallying had been at the hands of Australian driver/manager Wayne Bell. He launched Hyundai's WRC debut in New Zealand 1997 with the front-wheel drive Coupe, but his event spluttered to a halt with electrical failure as he attempted to leave parc ferme after only one stage.

Team-mate Bob Nicoli did complete the event, however, albeit in a lowly 24th place. He actually finished third in the F2 category behind Oriol Gomez in a SEAT and the equally new Suzuki Baleno of 'Monster' Tajima, but it would have been fifth had one car not retired three stages from home and another after the finish of the final stage.

Early attempts by Hyundai to break into the big time were thwarted to some extent by the geographical location of Bell's operation. Without a massive budget or, crucially at this stage, a commitment to the full championship, Hyundai's rally activities were of necessity confined to events in the Asia-Pacific region.

So it was hard to evaluate the progress, if any, that was being made and it was only when the WRC circus hit town in New Zealand or Australia that Bell could see for himself how things were going. It also has to be said that anyone developing a car for himself tends to head down a dangerous cul-de-sac where outright competitiveness is all too frequently blunted.

By the following year Bell had been joined by ex-Subaru driver Kenneth Eriksson, the Swede returning to a formula that had been very much his forte in his early career. In New Zealand Bell crashed out of the event at the end of day two, but Eriksson took third in F2 behind the two works SEATs and this time the car was well ahead of Tajima's Suzuki.

Behind the scenes, however, things were changing. A few weeks before Portugal that year, MSD had taken delivery of the competition package. Hyundai had realised that a European base was the only way to go if it was to become a serious player. At the time MSD was very much a touring car outfit, but its roots lay in rallying, notably with front-drive Opels but also with some four-wheel drive development experience.

The early events showed that the Coupe had potential, but that a lot of work was needed if it was to hold a candle to the established stars. Eriksson revelled in his new role and Alister McRae also seized a golden opportunity to step into the World arena along with his front-running brother.

Gradually the car evolved from a 'brick-like'

THE VIPS

DAVID WHITEHEAD

Whitehead's origins lie in the Dealer Opel Team set-up that was a major player in mid-70s British rallying. He set up Motor Sport Developments in 1991 and, seven years later, took over the Hyundai motorsport contract.

NICK CLIPSON

Clipson worked on the design of the Panther Solo and Jaguar XJ220 supercars before Volvo's touring car project. He joined MSD in 1998 and headed the Hyundai Accent WRC design team from 1999.

Nick Clipson is the man with the technical responsibility for the Accent WRC project.

beast into something considerably more sleek under the design pen of Peter Stevenson, the man behind Subaru's Impreza WRC styling. With the wider and lower shape came greater competitiveness, but there was another reason for the facelift.

All along Hyundai had wanted to get into the premier league but felt that it didn't have a car/engine package that was suitable. However, a chance meeting in New Zealand between Hyundai's motorsport chief GH Choi

and the FIA's technical delegate Jacques Berger led to the World Rally Car rules being clearly explained. Hyundai picked up on the possibilities and a plan was formed. By the end of 1998 the team had received the go-ahead to evaluate a World Rally Car project to take on the rest of the world, head to head.

The Coupe was the initial choice for the World Rally Car, but market forces overtook the plans. The new-shape Accent was due for release at the end of 1999 and so the decision was taken to delay the car's debut until everything could be designed into the new car. By the autumn of 1999 it was ready for testing and the team confirmed that Eriksson and McRae would be the driving squad for 2000.

Hyundai opted to miss Monte Carlo and the Safari because both required too much specialist knowledge for a new team and a new car. Budget constraints also reduced the amount of testing available and so much of the initial work was carried out in public, with inevitable trauma when things went wrong. Amid the frustration, however, there was also plenty to be pleased about. Argentina brought the team's first points and New Zealand its first stage win (crucially against serious opposition at that point in the event).

All in all it wasn't a bad first year for everyone concerned and there is plenty to suggest that 2001 will see a continuation on the upward curve.

David Whitehead's vast experience has been a valuable asset to the Hyundai team.

FOR THE RECORD

Country of origin: Korea
Team base: Milton Keynes, England
Date of formation: 1998 (MSD)
WRC debut: New Zealand 1997
WRC wins: 0

Team specification

Car: Hyundai Accent WRC **Tyres:** Michelin
Sponsors: Castrol **Team principal:** David Whitehead
Team manager: Paul Risbridger **Designer:** Nick Clipson

KENNETH ERIKSSON

Kenneth Eriksson is second only to Juha Kankkunen in terms of years at the top. The SuperSwede is well behind on points, but he's packed a lot into his career and there's no sign of his stopping just yet.

A WRC veteran of two decades, Eriksson's experience has been a vital ingredient.

Eriksson is a man of contrasts. In between blasting a rally car through the forests quicker than the vast majority of his fellow countrymen could imagine, he is equally likely to be found wandering in those same forests searching for peace and solitude.

Apart from once holding a World distance record for driving a car balanced on two wheels, Eriksson's greatest claim to fame is that he was the first and only winner of the FIA Group A World Championship.

From his first appearance on a World Championship event, Eriksson kept his programme to a minimum. Six attempts at his native Swedish Rally and one at Britain's RAC were all he had to look back on before he switched from the busy Opel Team Sweden camp to Volkswagen's factory team in 1986.

After finishing a creditable ninth on the Monte Carlo Rally he went to Sweden where he equalled his best result to that point, seventh. This time, however, it was achieved in spectacular style. With freshly fallen thick snow covering the ice on the stages there should have been no way that the front drive VW Golf could take on the four-wheel drive Lancias and Mazdas that were dominating the early days of the new Group A World Championship. But he set seven fastest times along the way – something that only event winner Timo Salonen could better. Later that same season Eriksson scored Volkswagen's one and only World Rally win, toppling a much-depleted field on the little-loved Ivory Coast Rally.

Eriksson's next career move was to Toyota in 1988 for a couple of seasons before he was off again in 1990 to Mitsubishi, where he would stay for the next six seasons. He picked up three wins along the way, including an emotional first Swedish Rally win in 1991 and a controversial second one in 1995, when team orders forced new boy Tommi Makinen to give up the lead amid a blizzard that struck the final day.

Having finished third in the World Championship, Eriksson departed Mitsubishi for Subaru at the end of that season but took with him the Asia-Pacific crown. In his two full seasons at Subaru, Eriksson added two more Asia-Pacific titles to his record and won his third Swedish Rally and his first in New Zealand (both in 1997).

He contested the 1998 Swedish Rally for Subaru but was then immediately released from his contract because he was then very much the third-string driver behind Colin McRae and Piero Liatti. Hyundai needed an experienced driver and so Eriksson immediately stepped aboard the Coupe, insisting that it was not a step backwards to his roots but a step forward, because he could help develop both a new car and a new team. Although frustrated at the lack of test time, Eriksson seems happier now than for some while.

STAGE NOTES

Nationality: Swedish
Born: May 13, 1956, Appelbo, Sweden
Teams: Saab 1980–1982, Opel 1983–1985, Volkswagen 1986–1987, Toyota 1988–1989, Mitsubishi 1990–1995, Subaru 1996–1998, Hyundai 1999–

Career record

First rally: 1977 with Saab 96
WRC debut: 1980 Swedish Rally (Saab 96V4, 51o/a)
WRC starts: 116
WRC wins: 6
1987 Ivory Coast; 1991 Swedish; 1995 Swedish, Australia; 1997 Swedish, New Zealand.
Stage wins: 214
Honours: 1986 Group A World Champion, 1995-1997 FIA Asia-Pacific Champion

ALISTER McRae

If Richard Burns is upset at having to follow in the footsteps of Colin McRae then spare a thought for Alister, Colin's younger brother! Yet despite taking a while to break into the big time, Alister is proving to be much in demand.

Colin McRae's style is to throw the car at a corner and then sort things out, while Alister is much more of a 'thinking' driver. As a result it was Colin who got the initial attention, leaving Alister to pick up the pieces. He had a sniff of the big time in the early 1990s when he became British Group N Champion with a semi-official Ford, before going on to win the championship outright in 1995 with a Nissan Sunny.

In that period he tackled a string of World Championship events, including the 1994 Indonesia Rally in an Motor Sport Developments-run Vauxhall Calibra, an event that would stand him in good stead when MSD needed drivers for its Hyundai project a few seasons later.

In the 1993 season, he was paired with Burns in a two-car Subaru team on the British Championship. A few decent results came his way, but he was generally overshadowed by Burns, who was out to take revenge on McRae for denying him the Group N drive the previous season following the successful Shell Scholarship programme.

While Burns moved on from his 1993 series win into the full Subaru team, McRae's chance seemed to slip him by and for a while it looked like his career would be blighted by the same frustrations that had denied his father, Jimmy, a real crack at a top drive.

Until 1999, the bulk of McRae's World Championship experience came primarily from his days with Nissan and Volkswagen, where he took Formula 2 victory on many occasions. To date, however, his best overall placing on a World Rally event was when he finished fourth, behind a trio of Subarus, on the 1995 RAC Rally – where victory was enough for Colin to clinch the championship.

McRae was an occasional driver for Hyundai in 1998 before joining the team full time the following season. The McRae family has had close ties to the MSD management for nearly 25 years and so he was certainly no unknown

STAGE NOTES

Nationality: Scottish
Born: December 20, 1970, Lanark, Scotland
Teams: Subaru 1991, Ford 1992, Ford/Subaru 1993, Nissan 1994-1995, Volkswagen 1996-1998, Hyundai 1998 (part)-

Career record

First rally: 1988 with Ford Escort
WRC debut: 1991 Rally GB (Subaru Legacy RS, engine failure)
WRC starts: 42
WRC wins: 0
Stage wins: 4
Honours: 1992 British Group N Champion, 1995 British Champion.

quantity when the team needed a driver to partner Kenneth Eriksson.

McRae was not prepared to let what might be his best chance to date slip through his fingers. He gave the team its first F2 win in Portugal that year, and subsequently has moved seamlessly into the Accent WRC. That was the car in which the New Zealand Rally of 2000 brought Hyundai's first stage win, with Alister beating his brother in the process!

Alister has been involved with the Accent project from the outset but knows that it is at least a year away from a possible first victory. In the meantime, however, teams such as Peugeot spotted his potential and towards the end of 2000 there were strong suggestions that a move to France was on the cards.

Colin McRae is a tough act to follow, but brother Alister is making a decent fist of it.

MITSUBISHI

Playing the Game

Mitsubishi's motto is 'The Spirit of Competition' and, without a doubt, this is one team with its roots very firmly planted in an era where taking part was just as important as winning. But perhaps it is time to rethink that strategy.

When the FIA introduced the World Rally Car formula for the 1997 season there was a rush of technical development among all but one of the leading teams, each eager to embrace the new freedoms that the new rules offered. Mitsubishi is the one team that, four seasons down the line, has only just taken up the WRC option.

While the attraction of being able to take a fairly bland road car and turn it, by way of a kit of parts plucked from the company product range, into a world-beating rally car has its merits, Mitsubishi could sacrifice more than most by taking that route. For while the WRC formula means that there is no longer the need to build 25,000 high-priced, high-performance road cars before the competition version, it also means that there can be no Group N versions of the sport's leading machinery without that production figure.

For Mitsubishi this is a problem for, just behind the factory entries on any World Championship Rally, sits a phalanx of Group N cars, most of which are Mitsubishis. Quite simply, the Japanese giant can sell as many cars as it produces and there is no way that market forces will allow it to kill off this vital part of its programme.

Ironically, Mitsubishi is one of the few teams that take Group N seriously. Only Subaru – with a far weaker power base in the category – has made any serious development in the Group N arena, but it is still well short of Mitsubishi. Thanks to the strong Group N programme that underpins many of the Far East regional rally championships, Mitsubishi also has enjoyed great success on series such as the FIA's Asia-Pacific Championship.

However, without a doubt the restrictions imposed by sticking to tradition are starting to manifest themselves in the performance of the Lancer (badged as a Carisma for European markets) and last November Mitsubishi confirmed that it will debut a WRC car this autumn.

Nevertheless the Group A car has served Mitsubishi well. It sits comfortably with the sport's best in terms of wins. Although it has won the manufacturers' title only once, it has carried Tommi Makinen to a record-breaking four straight drivers' titles between 1996 and 1999.

The Lancer struggled to keep on the pace in 2000 and will be pensioned off in 2001.

THE VIPS

ANDREW COWAN

Duns-born Cowan was a successful former driver (he twice won the London-Sydney marathon) before taking up management with Mitsubishi. He's very much a gentleman player in a world of hard-nosed businessmen.

BERNARD LINDAUER

Lindauer left school, went straight into the suspension department of Renault's Formula One team, and never looked back. Subsequent engineering work at Peugeot, Mazda and Ford led him to Mitsubishi Ralliart in 1997.

Last year was a pretty lean affair for Makinen and Mitsubishi, not helped by a second season of lacklustre performances by the team's number two driver, Freddy Loix. There seems little doubt that his possession of a Mitsubishi Ralliart contract beyond the end of 2000 owed much to his bringing Marlboro money to the team from its enthusiastic Belgian arm.

Mitsubishi's early successes came at the Safari Rally, where Joginder Singh won the team's debut event in 1974 and repeated the feat two seasons later. The 1976 success marked a 1-2-3 for the team with the third-placed car driven by Andrew Cowan, now the team principal of Marlboro Mitsubishi Ralliart. For good measure, sixth place was taken by Kenjiro Shinozuka, who eventually went on to win both the 1991 and 1992 Ivory Coast rallies for the team.

It was another 13 years before Mitsubishi reappeared on the top step of the podium with victories in Finland (for Michael Ericsson) and surprisingly for Pentti Airikkala against much more favoured opposition on Britain's RAC Rally at the end of the 1989 season.

The return to form came with a car very different from the Colt Lancer of the mid-seventies. By now you needed four-wheel drive and a turbocharged 2-litre engine for success. The car used by Mitsubishi was the Galant VR-4, a cumbersome saloon and one that, in road trim, featured four-wheel steering.

The Galant was replaced for the start of the 1993 season by the lighter, and therefore far more suitable, Lancer model that is now heading for its seventh evolution version, before Mitsubishi finally introduces its World Rally Car.

Kenneth Eriksson enjoyed the early successes with the Lancer, but it was when Makinen joined the team for 1996 (after a mix-and-match year with Nissan and Ford in 1995) that Mitsubishi finally arrived on the rally map. Cowan had told his Japanese masters that if they gave him the budget to sign Makinen then he would deliver the World Championship. It was a promise that was quickly fulfilled (and repeated over the next three seasons as well, for good measure), but one that is becoming increasingly hard to maintain amid the growing competition that now marks the modern era.

In the championship's weaker moments, Mitsubishi was right up at the top of the tree. Now, with the pack containing four or five teams with serious victory potential, just taking part won't be enough. Winning is now everything.

Andrew Cowan was a respected driver long before he took up team management.

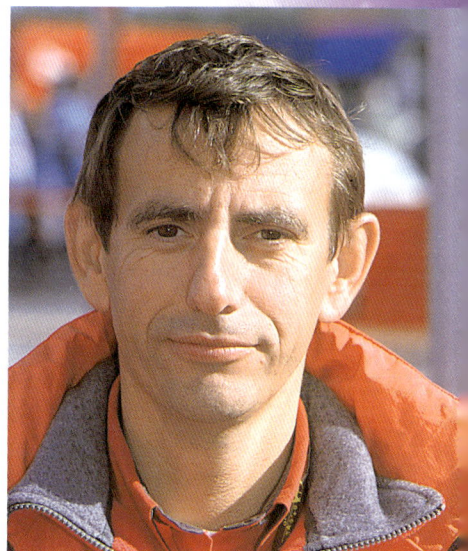

The arrival of a WRC Mitsubishi in 2001 will excite engineer Lindauer.

FOR THE RECORD

Country of origin: Japan **Team base:** Rugby, England
Date of formation: 1974 **WRC debut:** Safari 1974
First WRC win: Safari 1974 **WRC wins:** 31
Manufacturers titles: 1998
Drivers titles: 1996, 1997, 1998, 1999 (all Tommi Makinen)

Team specification

Car: Mitsubishi Lancer Evo/Carisma GT **Tyres:** Michelin
Sponsors: Marlboro **Team principal:** Andrew Cowan
Designer: Bernard Lindauer **Test driver:** Lasse Lampi

TOMMI MAKINEN

Tommi Makinen's 2000 season wasn't much to write home about, but having won the previous four World Championships, he already had staked a claim to the title of greatest driver ever, despite packing his main successes into only a five-year period.

His big break came with Mitsubishi at a time when his career seemed to be foundering. A dalliance with the World Championship in 1992 was curtailed when Nissan pulled the plug on its ill-starred programme, but in 1994 he was back with the Japanese team on a limited programme of World Championship events.

Despite this, his career was going nowhere. It all changed when Ford asked him to drive an Escort Cosworth on the 1,000 Lakes Rally and Makinen simply cruised to his first World Rally win.

Mitsubishi pounced for 1995, confident that his arrival would lead them to the World Championship. The season brought only one win, a virtually unchallenged success on the non-championship 1,000 Lakes. Easy though it was, the win set him on course for five consecutive home victories, a record that no other driver has matched. Only FIA Rallies Commission president Shekhar Mehta (with four successive Safari wins), has even gone close.

The following year was a very different picture, however. Makinen took five wins and his first World Championship. The title was clinched with his Australia victory, two events from the end of the season. By that point he had finished six rallies, won five, taken second once and retired only twice. It was a remarkable record of consistency, and one that would become a trademark in future years.

In 1997 Makinen only once finished outside the top three places. He needed at least sixth place on the final round, and he coaxed his ailing, flu-ridden body to sixth place in a sodden British finale, got the one point he needed and joined the elite

STAGE NOTES

Nationality: Finnish
Born: June 26, 1964, Puuppola, Finland
Teams: Lancia 1987–1989, Mitsubishi 1990, Nissan 1992, Nissan/Ford/Mitsubishi 1994, Mitsubishi 1995–

Career record

First rally: 1985 with Ford Escort RS2000
WRC debut: 1987 1000 Lakes (Lancia Delta HF 4WD, accident)
WRC starts: 97
WRC wins: 20
1994 Finland; 1996 Sweden, Safari, Argentina, Finland, Australia; 1997 Portugal, Catalunya, Argentina, Finland, San Remo, Australia; 1998 Sweden, Argentina, Finland, San Remo, Australia; 1999 Monte Carlo, Sweden, New Zealand, San Remo; 2000 Monte Carlo
Stage wins: 305
Honours: 1987 Finnish Champion, 1996-1999 World Rally Champion

club of back-to-back title winners.

Makinen again moved into the record books in 1998, despite a fairly slow start to the year by his standards. Nevertheless a run of three wins in Finland, San Remo and Australia brought a third successive title – a feat never before achieved. Only one thing now remained and that was to make it four, equalling the record set by the only other quadruple champion, Makinen's mentor Juha Kankkunen.

In bizarre circumstances, he made it. Carlos Sainz was on course for the title when his Toyota's engine blew only 500 metres from the end of the final stage of the final event. Makinen had retired on the opening day and was waiting for the cab to take him to the airport when the news came. With Sainz out, Makinen was king again.

Makinen's immediate future remains with Mitsubishi, but for how long? Unless the team can tune its current car, or build a radical new one, to match the performance of its rivals, Makinen may be on the move again. Some say to a new team, others suggest retirement. Only Makinen knows the answer to that one.

FREDDY LOIX

They call him Fast Freddy, but that nickname has looked something of a misnomer for most of the past two seasons. Only in Cyprus last year did the Belgian finally show the speed that made him hot property during his time at Toyota.

Freddy Loix grabbed people's attention when he started entering World Championship rallies with a Dealer Opel Team Belgium Astra in the early 1990s, but it wasn't until Toyota snared him in 1996 that he really began to blossom.

It was only through bad luck that he failed to turn winning ways on his home soil into similar results at World Championship level. Second place in Portugal 1997 and again at Catalunya 1998 were his best results, and he never quite pulled off that first big win.

During that period, however, he showed everybody that he was overawed neither by his rivals nor the events themselves. This was a driver very much on the move, especially as he was able to call on considerable support from Marlboro Belgium to back his campaign.

He made good use of the money to ensure that he was driving the best possible Corolla outside the factory team. When Toyota needed someone to deliver the goods in Catalunya 1998 (at a time when Didier Auriol's form was slumping), Loix was the man that the team bosses approached to do the business – hence that second place, ironically behind a rejuvenated Auriol!

Unfortunately there was little chance for Loix to establish himself as a regular team driver while Auriol and Carlos Sainz were at Toyota so, with the Marlboro money a useful bargaining tool, Loix set off to Rugby and joined Mitsubishi for 1999. The cars were repainted Marlboro red and all in the camp looked rosy.

Given his place in what was then the World Champion team, his subsequent slump in form has perhaps been more heavily criticised than it should. Remember, the 1999 season was Loix's first full year of World Championship rallying.

Crashing out of the Monte Carlo Rally on the opening stage (as Sainz had done) was not the most auspicious of starts. A lowly ninth place in Sweden, albeit on his first visit, did not help. Then came the high-speed flip that put him out of the Safari Rally and which did more damage than was first thought.

Loix was fortunate to survive the accident with nothing worse than cracked vertebrae and a one-event layoff, considering the way in which the car was wrecked. Since that shunt, however, his form hit rock bottom and it was a surprise when Mitsubishi renewed his contract towards the end of last year.

Solid, points-scoring finishes on the majority of his events look good enough on paper, but there have been times when even team leader Tommi Makinen seemed not to notice that there was another car in his party. Loix rediscovered himself in Cyprus last year, however, and there was a real feeling that he may have turned the corner. If so, then Mitsubishi will be a much stronger team this season.

Without Marlboro's support the future could have been bleak for Loix.

STAGE NOTES

Nationality: Belgian
Born: November 10, 1970, Tongeren, Belgium
Teams: Opel 1993–1995, Toyota 1996–1998, Mitsubishi 1999–

Career record

First rally: 1989 with Lancia HF Integrale
WRC debut: 1993 San Remo (Opel Astra GSi, 9o/a)
WRC starts: 45
WRC wins: 0
Stage wins: 28
Honours: Belgian Championship runner-up 1991

PEUGEOT

Without a doubt, Peugeot's return to the World Rally Championship was the move the establishment feared most. The new 206WRC proved immediately fast and, once the initial fragility was sorted out, it also proved to be a championship winner in pretty short order.

Peugeot has a long and rich history in the World Rally Championship, although it only really achieved its true potential during the Group B era of the early 1980s. Prior to that, Peugeot's best results came with the tank-like 504 saloon on endurance events such as the Safari and Morocco rallies.

Indeed, Peugeot's debut in the World Rally Championship was at the 1975 Safari where a 504, driven by Ove Andersson (now competitions boss at Toyota), took a debut win.

Later that same year Hannu Mikkola won in Morocco. His co-driver on that occasion was Jean Todt, who later went on to run Peugeot's successful rally effort before becoming Ferrari's F1 competitions manager.

Jean-Pierre Nicolas, who is the current Peugeot team manager, won the 1976 Morocco Rally in another 504, ahead of Simo Lampinen in the sister car. In 1978 the 504 was still winning, first on the Safari and then on the Ivory Coast rallies. Nicolas was the winning

driver on both those occasions: accompanied in the Safari win by Jean-Claude Lefebvre, who is now Peugeot's head of communications.

Without a doubt Peugeot has a long-standing reputation for being a starting point for anyone with a wish to make a career out of motorsport and it is a reputation that continues to this day. Both Colin McRae and Richard Burns got their first big breaks with Peugeot through an innovative one-make series that was a major part of the British scene in the late 1990s.

The 504 Coupe, however, was never going to be a match for the far more nimble cars that were dominating the championship at that time, and certainly had no answer to the four-wheel drive machinery that would become a prerequisite for success. Peugeot disappeared from the scene for a while but, when it returned in 1984, it did so with a real bang.

The intervening period had been one of major upheaval for the company. For a while the sporting arm was run under the banner of Talbot and netted the 1981 manufacturers' championship before the whole competition department was grouped together as Peugeot Talbot Sport. Jean Todt was now in overall command, aided by his enthusiastic English counterpart, Des O'Dell, who had overseen the Talbot end of the operation.

During 1983 Peugeot unveiled the 205 T16, arguably the world's first no-compromise Group B rally car. Stunning looks aside, it proved to have enormous potential. Up to this point Audi's brutal Quattro had enjoyed almost complete domination, its only rival being Lancia with its equally unattractive Delta S4. But could French chic overcome its rivals on the stages as readily as it had done in the showrooms?

The answer was undoubtedly in the affirmative. The car made its debut at the Corsica Rally in May of 1984 and was leading after only two stages. The dream debut wasn't

Peugeot was the team they all feared. And as the 2000 season proved, rightly so.

THE VIPS

JEAN-PIERRE NICOLAS

Nicolas has five WRC wins to his credit (among a host of other victories) and was the test driver for Peugeot's last WRC campaign two decades ago before turning to management.

MICHEL NANDAN

After initial work engineering rally and touring cars at Peugeot Italy, Nandan made his name at Toyota Team Europe in the early 90s before joining Peugeot Sport to create the 206WRC.

to be, however, and Ari Vatanen's car was left a burned-out wreck after it crashed off the road. Nevertheless, by the end of its debut season, Vatanen had given the car victories in Finland, San Remo and in Britain.

Over the next two seasons Timo Salonen and Juha Kankkunen respectively brought Peugeot both the drivers' and manufacturers' championships, with the rest barely getting a look in.

The tragic events of 1986 (three spectators killed in Portugal and Henri Toivonen crashing to a fiery death in Corsica) led the FIA to scrap the Group B category immediately. While most

Michel Nandan has turned the fragile 206 into a champion.

accepted that the cars, that now boasted anything from 500-600bhp, were too dangerous, Todt would not bow down. Peugeot withdrew from the championship, modified the 205s into desert racers and hillclimb specials, then set about winning events such as the trans-Sahara Paris-Dakar and the Pikes Peak hill climb in Colorado, USA.

Eventually Peugeot returned to the World Championship, although it was initially with the 306 kit car at the start of 1996, when Francois Delecour took second place on the non-championship Monte Carlo Rally. During the following year an evolution version of this incredibly wide machine was created and, thanks to lighter weight limits, proved to be capable of outrunning the factory cars on asphalt events. That it was beating them was cause enough for serious acrimony. Had it actually proved consistent enough to go on and win the champ-ionship there would have been real fireworks!

Meanwhile Peugeot was creating the 206 WRC and, at the Paris Motor Show of 1998, it was unveiled for the first time. During 1999 it cut its teeth on a limited programme of events and in 2000 shot immediately to the fore as a title contender and, ultimately, champion.

The 206 WRC, nimble, easy to drive and hugely competitive, was now equally as good as its 205 predecessor had been some 15 years earlier. The Peugeot lion has clearly lost none of its roar.

Jean-Pierre Nicolas has steered Peugeot back to the top in just one season.

FOR THE RECORD

Country of origin: France
Team base: Velizy, France
Date of formation: 1982 (Peugeot Sport)
WRC debut: Safari 1975
First WRC win: Safari 1975
WRC wins: 27 **Manufacturers titles:** 1985, 1986, 2000
Drivers titles: 1985 (Timo Salonen), 1986 (Juha Kankkunen), 2000 (Marcus Gronholm)

Team specification

Car: Peugeot 206WRC **Tyres:** Michelin
Sponsors: Esso, Clarion **Team principal:** Corrado Provera
Team manager: Jean-Pierre Nicolas **Designer:** Michel Nandan

DIDIER AURIOL

Didier Auriol must wonder who he has upset. Twice in the past two seasons he's had works drives pulled from beneath his feet. He knows time is running out but he's determined to enjoy the twilight of his career with a move to Peugeot.

French driver, French team. Will 2001 see a fresh start for Didier Auriol?

The fates haven't been too kind to Auriol. With 19 World Championship wins to his credit he was only four adrift of Juha Kankkunen's all-time record when he won in China two seasons ago. Suddenly, however, things went awry for the little Frenchman.

Within a few weeks of his success on the one and only Chinese round of the World Championship, Toyota confirmed it was pulling out of rallying to crank up its Formula 1 project. While team-mate Carlos Sainz renewed his links with Ford, Auriol headed for Barcelona and a SEAT team desperate for an established star.

Auriol knew what was needed in a winning car but SEAT couldn't provide it, and by the autumn of last year he was openly considering declining the second year of his contract. However, instead of possibly leaving SEAT on his own terms, SEAT followed Toyota's suit in scrapping its rally programme for the following season and Auriol found himself at the job centre instead.

At 42 Auriol doesn't have the benefit of youth on his side. In Cyprus, days after the SEAT announcement, he confessed that he needed to get into a winning car. It was too late, he said, to wait to see what came along. He had to act fast and the best options seemingly available were a switch to Peugeot (with whom he'd had negotiations on and off for three seasons) and Citroen, whose Xsara T4 prototype has proved stunningly quick.

Auriol, along with Sainz, established European drivers' credentials throughout the mid-nineties. They proved that the Scandinavians could be beaten, never more so by being the only two non-Scandinavians to win Finland's 1000 Lakes Rally. While Sainz set the pace and took two World Championships, however, Auriol had to wait until 1994 before landing his lone success.

The former ambulance driver had made his name with Ford in the mid-eighties, as did Sainz. And at the same time as Sainz left for Toyota's four-wheel drive opportunities, Auriol departed for Lancia. Then, when Lancia withdrew (a familiar theme for Auriol) he found a home at Toyota and achieved his dream. It compensated for a bizarre 1992 season when his Lancia won a record six times from 10 starts but lost the World Championship thanks to a broken plug lead on the final round in Britain.

Rallying demands versatility and this hasn't always sat easily with Auriol. If the car is perfect then he's as quick as anyone but, if it's not, he can slip away from the leaders very quickly indeed. Perhaps the mental battle is the one area where he has let himself down more than necessary but he still remains in the top group of drivers. At Peugeot he now has a car in which to prove it.

STAGE NOTES

Nationality: French
Born: August 18, 1958, Montpellier, France
Teams: Renault 1984-1985, Austin Rover 1986, Ford 1987-1988, Lancia 1989-1992, Toyota 1993-1999, (Subaru/Mitsubishi1996), SEAT 2000; Peugeot 2001–

Career record

First rally: 1979 with Simca Rallye 2
WRC debut: 1984 Corsica Rally (Renault 5 Turbo, retired)
WRC starts: 122
WRC wins: 19
1988 Corsica; 1989 Corsica; 1990 Monte Carlo, Corsica, San Remo; 1991 San Remo; 1992 Monte Carlo, Corsica, Acropolis, Argentina, Finland, Australia; 1993 Monte Carlo; 1994 Corsica, Argentina, San Remo; 1995 Corsica; 1998 Catalunya; 1999 China.
Stage wins: 538
Honours: 1986-1988 French Champion, 1994 World Champion

MARCUS GRONHOLM

Marcus Gronholm has been the revelation of the new millennium. After several false starts with factory teams he finally got his act together with Peugeot and turned a partial programme into a convincing World Drivers' Championship title.

Ulf Gronholm may have been a legend in Finnish rallying, but his son Marcus has outshone him. However, for years it seemed as though this lanky Finn was destined to be the guy who had the breaks but who could never make full use of them.

He is a four-time Finnish champion, usually sharing the success with his cousin Sebastian Lindholm, who got his first big factory drive in 1992. On that occasion Toyota signed him up for the 1000 Lakes Rally. It was a case of too much too soon and after sharing fastest time with his vastly more experienced team-mate Markku Alen on the opening stage, he crashed and was withdrawn.

Gronholm stayed loyal to the marque, however, and used a string of ex-works Celicas as they became available to rack up his domestic titles. Tellingly, his World Championship experience was confined to the Swedish and Finnish rounds until he added Portugal and New Zealand in 1995, six years after his series debut.

A wider programme (albeit still privately funded) kicked in for 1997 where, in addition to Sweden, he competed again in Portugal and then Argentina. By the time Finland came round he was back in a factory Toyota, helping the team to return from its FIA-imposed exile following the turbo-cheating scandal of 1995.

Gronholm gave the Corolla World Rally car its world debut on a domestic event before getting the keys again for its WRC debut on the 1000 Lakes. Both car and driver proved quick, leading at the end of the first day before being overhauled and finally retiring with fuel problems two stages from home.

Gronholm was back in favour and, while regular places in the team were not available, he did enough in a semi-works car to attract attention. Seventh place in 1998 on his home event, after another blistering start, brought a flood of offers and within weeks he was confirmed as a Peugeot driver for 1999.

His role was to underpin the efforts of Francois Delecour and Gilles Panizzi, but as the 2000 season unfolded, Gronholm proved to be the star and a limited programme was quickly expanded as he became a title contender.

Wins in Sweden and New Zealand (coupled with second places in Portugal and Argentina) brought him right into the reckoning for the championship and a crushing victory in his home event, took him into the series lead. Only his lack of previous experience of many events was keeping him from running away with the crown. The prize came with a superbly controlled drive in Britain on the season's finale. Gronholm certainly was ensuring that Finns really are what they used to be...

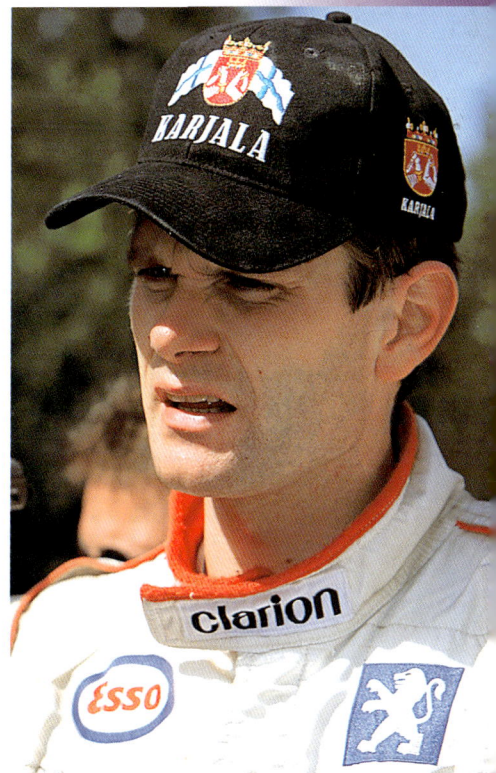

Marcus Gronholm was the star of the 2000 season, champion at his first attempt.

STAGE NOTES

Nationality: Finnish
Born: February 5, 1968, Espoo, Finland
Teams: Toyota 1990–1998, (SEAT/Mitsubishi drives in 1999), Peugeot 1999–

Career record

First rally: 1987 with Ford Escort 1300
WRC debut: 1989 1000 Lakes (Lancia Delta HF Integrale, 23 o/a)
WRC starts: 44
WRC wins: 4
2000 Sweden, New Zealand, Finland, Australia
Stage wins: 62
Honours: 1989 Scandinavian Champion, 1994 & 1996-1998 Finnish Champion, 2000 World Champion

SKODA
Bouncing Czechs

They used to laugh about Skoda, but not any more. The image has changed since being incorporated into the Volkswagen-Audi Group and motorsport has been a useful canvas on which to paint a fresh picture. But Skoda has been around longer than most.

Building a winning car on a tiny budget is Dietmar Metrich's task.

Pavel Janeba is steering Skoda towards the top, step by step.

Skoda has been a serious player at the top level of motorsport since the start of 1999, when it introduced the Octavia WRC at Monte Carlo. However, you can go back 63 years and find Skodas taking class wins on that same Monte Carlo Rally. This is a company with a rich motorsport heritage.

To be fair, though, Skoda has based its past on strength and reliability. With a customer base well away from cash-rich western Europe, the Czech team had to cut its cloth by necessity according to the relevant market, hence a string of basic cars that ran for ever was the product range on offer.

But those basic cars, often fairly ugly ones at that, racked up class win after class win. Not against zero opposition either, for the 1300cc category has underpinned many top-flight events thanks to the emergence of the small hatchback market.

Although Skoda has dallied briefly with sportscar racing and even Formula 3, it is rallying that has given the company its greatest success. A whole run of rear-engined cars throughout the 1970s and most of the 1980s added to Skoda's glorious history and the team was especially proud to take 25 class wins in 25 years on Britain's RAC Rally (usually with Norwegian driver John Haugland at the wheel) during that period. If the team happened to miss a year it simply entered two classes the next time round to balance the figures again!

They may not have had the most high-tech facilities or equipment, but Skoda certainly had the enthusiasm. With the Cold War and the Iron Curtain very much a reality during the majority of Skoda's past, the opportunity to leave the country and see the world was eagerly sought, and it was considered a major incentive to work hard and become part of the rally team.

Happily things are much freer these days and with western influence the team has made huge strides in the past few seasons.

In 1989 Skoda abandoned the familiar rear-engined cars for the front-engined and front-wheel drive Favorit, albeit still with only 1300cc. Class wins continued to fall to the team, but its finest hour was in 1994 when, competing in the second FIA 2-litre Cup against more powerful opposition, Skoda became World Champions.

The following year the Favorit evolved into the Felicia and in 1996 Stig Blomqvist took one of these amazing little cars to third overall on an ice-bound RAC Rally, admittedly in the event's one-year sabbatical from the world championship.

The Octavia WRC project was authorised that same year following the FIA's creation of the World Rally Car concept from 1997.

FOR THE RECORD

Country of origin: Czechoslovakia
Team base: Mlada Boleslav, Czechoslovakia
Date of formation: 1969   **WRC debut:** RAC Rally 1974
WRC wins: 0   **Manufacturers titles:** 1994 FIA 2-litre Cup

Team specification

Car: Skoda Octavia WRC   **Tyres:** Michelin   **Sponsors:** Castrol   **Team principal:** Pavel Janeba   **Designer:** Dietmar Metrich

THE VIPS

PAVEL JANEBA

A former successful Skoda driver, Janeba has masterminded Skoda's rise to fame. Janeba's team won the 1994 World 2-litre crown with a pair of 1300cc Favorits and is now progressing with the Octavia WRC.

DIETMAR METRICH

Metrich joined Skoda from Mitsubishi Ralliart Germany in 1998 after winning two Group N World Championships and his considerable experience, particularly with turbo engines and four-wheel drive, has been vital factor in the Octavia programme.

Without a 2-litre turbocharged four-wheel drive car on its books there was no other way that Skoda could countenance such a step up, but the WRC rules now permitted teams such as Skoda to buy in technology.

Prodrive's engineering division did a lot of the ground work while Skoda ran a front-wheel drive version of the big saloon for a couple of seasons, including a Formula 2 category win on the 1998 European Championship for team driver Emil Triner.

The four-wheel drive car made its debut on the 1999 Monte Carlo Rally, but you might have been forgiven for not noticing. Delays in sorting the engine meant that the team arrived ill-prepared and both cars were out before a

Consistency is starting to turn into competitiveness for the Czech team.

stage had begun. German driver Armin Schwarz had been a crucial appointment to the team (due to a wealth of experience), but his clutch failed on the run from the harbour parc ferme to the start ramp at Casino Square. Pavel Sibera's car only got as far as the first service park before it was also withdrawn with power-steering failure.

The 1999 car was a basic affair and was designed as a learning platform. Over the course of the season the team built reliability into the Octavia, followed by improved performance.

In 2000 the team abandoned its rigid policy of having at least one Czech driver on the team and added Spain's Luis Climent to the line-up alongside Schwarz. It wasn't Skoda's finest move, because although the Valencia driver brought vital extra finance, he was never competitive and was dropped for the 2001 season.

It will take a few more seasons before Skoda can seriously challenge for outright honours but, during 2000, the team showed that its legendary points-scoring abilities had not been compromised in the step up to premier league level. By the summer Skoda was briefly ahead of its more established VAG stablemate SEAT and consistency was starting to turn into competitiveness with every event.

Skoda for World Champion? Not just yet, but maybe it's not a joke either.

ARMIN SCHWARZ

They say you make your own luck. If true, Armin Schwarz is probably one of the more self-destructive drivers around. Undoubtedly quick, definitely likeable ... but Schwarz has never quite fulfilled his potential. Perhaps he's just been too impatient for success.

Armin Schwarz has often knocked on the door of success, but it won't open.

He burst onto the scene in 1988, taking the big and cumbersome Audi 200 Quattro to an astonishing fifth overall on Britain's RAC Rally, his World Championship debut. As a protégé of the great Walter Rohrl, Schwarz emerged from the now virtually defunct German rally scene and looked set for stardom.

His career continued through the following season, still with the Schmidt Motorsport-run Audi, but aside from a couple of top-ten places, the season yielded little but experience for the young German. It was hardly surprising, though, for the car was singularly unsuited to anything but endurance events. Its 1987 Safari Rally win, in the hands of Hannu Mikkola, was its only WRC success (and Audi's last).

Schwarz's efforts had not gone unnoticed, however, and the Cologne-based Toyota Team Europe signed him up for the next three seasons. Although the partnership yielded his one and only World Championship rally win (Catalunya 1991), it didn't produce too many great drives and all but one of his eight retirements during his Toyota days were because of accidents.

Unlike Rohrl, Schwarz is an aggressive driver and there are many tales over the years of seeing him with at least one wheel in a ditch as he tried to wring the last ounce of performance from a car. Unfortunately too many of those ditches contained rocks that ultimately led to his downfall.

Schwarz joined Mitsubishi for a couple of seasons before returning to Toyota for what would prove to be the fateful 1995 season. He already had crashed out of the Catalunya event and was therefore spared the embarrassment of exclusion when the scrutineers found Toyota's ingenious but highly illegal system to circumvent the turbo air restrictor.

Although the factory team was banned from competing in 1996, several private operations continued and so Schwarz stayed with Toyota, embarked on a programme of European Championship events and clinched the crown. By way of a lap of honour, Schwarz brought the winning car to Britain's RAC Rally (in its non-championship year) and defied the elements to win a snow-and-ice-bound event that had destroyed the hopes of many star names.

Ford issued call-up papers to Schwarz for 1997 and, for the first few events, his tenacity and engineering skills kept the team in the points far more often that it might have deserved. Arguments over contracts, however, led to his being dismissed after Corsica. Meanwhile, Skoda needed an experienced driver to lead its World Rally Car project. Schwarz signed in 1999 and, despite some early teething troubles, he has been a solid and committed worker. It may be a while before he has a chance to improve his victory total, but a surprise fastest time on last year's Catalunya Rally showed he's lost none of his attacking form.

STAGE NOTES

Nationality: German
Born: July 16, 1963, Oberreichenbach, Germany
Teams: Audi 1988–1989, Toyota 1990–1992, 1995–1996, Mitsubishi 1993–1994, Ford 1997–1998, Skoda 1999–

Career record

First rally: 1983 with Fiat 131
WRC debut: 1988 Rally GB (Audi 200 Quattro, 5o/a)
WRC starts: 61
WRC wins: 1
1991 Catalunya
Stage wins: 96
Honours: 1987 & 1988 German Champion, 1996 European Champion

BRUNO THIRY

The affable Belgian is arguably the most unlucky driver in World rallying. He came within a whisker of winning the 1995 Corsica Rally but has never been as close since. A Skoda deal for 2001 may give him an unexpected career boost.

It is sad to think that Bruno Thiry is best remembered for failing to win the 1995 Corsica Rally but his public humiliation is an image that tends to stick in the mind. At the time the sport was going through a painful transition with regard to servicing rules and the current Service Park solution hadn't been dreamed up. In 1995 the usual scenario was that drivers completed pairs of stages with no service in between the two.

Thiry was leading the event with two stages to go but broke a wheel bearing on his Ford Escort Cosworth on the penultimate test. Despite the no-service zone before the final stage, access to the place was simple and many of his team mechanics were there to urge him on for one final time. Instead they could do nothing but stand around, full of expertise but helpless to act.

Thiry took a long time to recover from the mental blow and it is of little consequence that this one incident probably did more to encourage a rethink of the rules than any of the hours spent by the rule makers in meetings.

Thiry came to the attention of the big teams by his successes in Belgium, and then on the World stage, at the wheel of an Opel Astra. His best result was second overall on the Ivory Coast Rally of 1992 although the paucity of support for the second rate African event painted a false picture of the achievement. He helped the GM Europe team to the first ever FIA 2-litre Cup (unofficially titled the Formula 2 World Championship) in 1993 and that set him up for a factory drive in the Ford team, albeit at a time when it was entering a period of huge instability.

His final year at the original Ford team (before the programme was taken away from Boreham and shifted to Malcolm Wilson's Cumbria base) netted third places in San Remo and Catalunya before he added another podium place for the 'new' Ford team on the 1998 Rally of Great Britain.

Thiry landed a Subaru drive in 1999 but it was cut short after a silly accident in Corsica. He sat on the sidelines for some time before Skoda asked him to drive the Octavia WRC on that year's Rally GB. Thiry was a star, finishing fourth to give the car its best ever result on a WRC event but it was still not enough to land a contract for 2000. Instead, Thiry tackled a selection of events for Citroen, taking the Xsara kit car to the European F2 title while Luis Climent wasted the second Skoda seat for most of the year.

Thiry's deal for 2001 was confirmed just before last year's Rally GB and completes the team's line-up for its most ambitious programme to date.

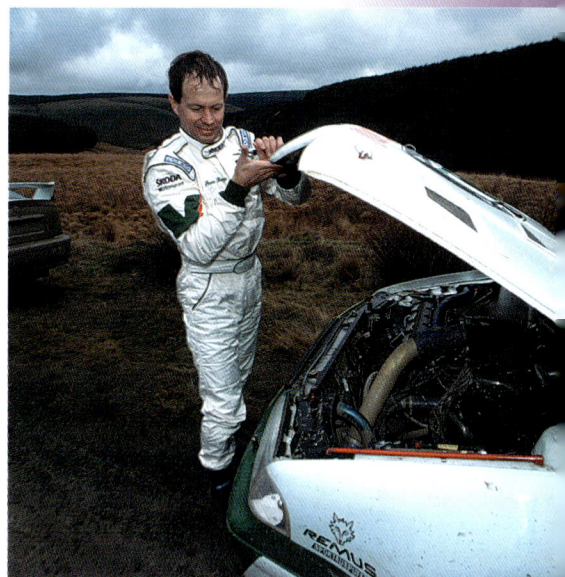
Mechanical problems have often upset Thiry's dreams, but he regularly bounces back.

STAGE NOTES

Nationality: Belgian
Born: October 8, 1962, St Vith, Belgium
Teams: Opel 1991–1993, Ford 1994–1998, Subaru/Skoda 1999, Citroen 2000, Skoda 2001–

Career record

First rally: 1981 with Simca Rallye
WRC debut: 1989 Britain (Audi 90 Quattro, 13o/a)
WRC starts: 54
WRC wins: 0
Stage wins: 39
Honours: Led GM Europe to inaugural FIA 2-litre Cup in 1993; European F2 Champion 2000 with Citroen

SUBARU
The Style Council

Image is everything to Subaru and even in the team's darkest seasons the seven stars of the team logo have stood out like a beacon. Flash headquarters, flash hospitality and one of the most stylish cars in the pack. That's Subaru.

After a couple of years treading water, Subaru bounced back to competitiveness in 2000. In the past few seasons the opening months of the championship have been largely a waste of time with precious few points coming the way of either team or drivers. Traditionally it has been the events held in the second half of the year where the team's star has truly shone.

One always felt, however, that if Subaru could string together a good start to the year then the late season game of 'catch-up' might turn into a title challenge worthy of the name – and would bring the team back to the position it enjoyed in the mid-1990s.

One of the problem areas in recent seasons has been the team's performance on asphalt. Although Corsica was never too much of a drama, Catalunya and San Remo were disasters.

The winter 'break' (all of eight weeks including Christmas and the Millennium celebrations) between the end of the 1999

A mid-season hiatus cost Subaru any chance of the 2000 title.

season and the start of the new year contained frantic activity and this time the effort appears to have paid off.

A calendar reshuffle meant that the bulk of the asphalt competition shifted later in the season, but Catalunya remained in March and Subaru simply flew over the Spanish tarmac. By then Richard Burns had already won the Safari Rally and gone on to record a debut win for the Impreza WRC2000 in Portugal, and so second place in Spain was a good way to consolidate his championship lead. And this was no distant second either. Burns battled with arch-rival Colin McRae for every scrap right to the final finish line with the pair just seconds apart.

This was surely going to be Burns's year. The flame-haired Cotswold's driver was maturing rapidly and was now a clear favourite for just about every event he started. Monte Carlo remains a difficult event for him, Sweden is still a bit of a lottery as well but after that he is in a class of his own.

Safari was a dominant performance, Portugal just as much so once the early skirmishes were out of the way. Argentina, a third gravel win in succession, was hard fought over the first two days and Burns went into the Acropolis, New Zealand, Finland and Cyprus quartet brimming with confidence. Mechanical gremlins halted him on the first two events, however, and a high-speed accident in Finland brought up a third no-score to let Marcus Gronholm through into the series lead. It certainly ensured that the championship was not going to be a walkover for whoever took the crown.

To many people Subaru represents the nouveau riche of rallying. The Anglo-Japanese marriage of Banbury-based Prodrive and the Tokyo-based Fuji Heavy Industries has created rallying's equivalent of the McLaren Formula One team and an outfit that surely leads the way in both technology and innovation.

DAVID RICHARDS

Founder, chairman and driving force behind Prodrive. This former co-driver (he won the 1981 WRC alongside Ari Vatanen) now drives rallying's global TV expansion and has stepped back from the 'hands-on' running of the team.

DAVID LAPWORTH

Prodrive's technical director and Subaru team manager will always be credited as the man who turned Subaru's farmers' runabout into a World Rally Championship supercar with soaring sales figures and brand image.

In the decade that has passed since Markku Alen debuted the relatively cumbersome Legacy RS on the Acropolis Rally of 1990, Prodrive has honed the Japanese cars not only into World Championship winning machinery, but also highly desirable road cars. Once the domain of farmers alone, Subaru is now one of the world's great road cars and it has risen to this position solely on the back of the rally programme.

Initially this came through back-to-back British titles for Colin McRae (in 1991 and 1992 with Richard Burns adding the 1993 crown for good measure) before McRae moved on to the World stage and started winning there as well.

From the Legacy, Subaru switched to the

David Lapworth has engineered Subaru's rise to fame.

much more nimble Impreza and results came thick and fast. McRae's New Zealand win of 1993 in the Legacy made history as the first WRC win for Subaru and the first for a British driver since Roger Clark's 1976 RAC Rally success. He repeated the result in 1994 with the Impreza (close behind Carlos Sainz's Acropolis success, the first for the new model) and his Kiwi hat-trick came in the middle of what would become a championship winning season as McRae became Britain's first World Rally Champion. At the same time Subaru notched the first of three successive Manufacturers' titles.

The FIA's new World Rally Car formula was embraced wholeheartedly by Prodrive on Subaru's behalf and at the end of 1996, amid a typically slick presentation, Subaru unveiled the first car for the new formula.

The stunning Impreza WRC97 debuted at the 1997 Monte Carlo Rally and, in the hands of Piero Liatti, won rallying's Blue Riband event. Since then the car has been updated every year and while it may look the same from the outside, the WRC2000 bears no other technological resemblance to the WRC97.

Another new Impreza is expected to debut in Monte Carlo 2001 and the team's commitment to a youth policy could ensure that the Subaru name continues at the top for many more seasons to come.

Although he has moved on to other projects, David Richards remains a figurehead.

FOR THE RECORD

Country of origin: Japan
Team base: Banbury, England
Date of formation: 1989
WRC debut: 1990 Acropolis Rally
First WRC win: 1993 New Zealand Rally
WRC wins: 32
Manufacturers titles: 1995, 1996, 1997
Drivers titles: 1995 (Colin McRae)

Team specification

Car: Subaru Impreza WRC **Tyres:** Pirelli
Sponsors: Pirelli, Sparco **Team principal:** David Richards
Team manager: John Spiller **Designer:** David Lapworth
Test driver: Robbie Head

RICHARD BURNS

For most of his career Richard Burns has laboured in the shadow of British rival Colin McRae, but in 2000 Burns finally emerged from that shadow as a top-line driver and was a World Rally Championship contender in his own right.

Richard Burns has twice been the championship runner-up. Third time lucky?

Given that Burns followed McRae's path from early days with two-wheel drive Peugeots, to a first big break with Subaru and then on to the World Championship, where both took their first major success in New Zealand, comparisons have always been drawn between the pair.

It is a situation that has not always sat easily with Burns, the flame-haired driver from Stow on the Wold, and at times he has appeared to have a chip on his shoulder about the matter. In 2000, however, there is little question that he has emerged from McRae's shadow in more ways than one.

Never the most demonstrative driver, Burns has racked up his achievements through meticulous preparation and a run of consistency that is awesome in its relentless passage. Only during his time with Mitsubishi, when he broke free from the Subaru shackles in a bid to increase his standing in the sport as the team's lead entry on the second-string Asia-Pacific Championship, did this consistency fail him. Quite simply the title was his for the taking, but he tried too hard too soon and was denied the prize through a run of non-finishes.

His driving style would grace a race track because he is the master of the smooth line, not one of life's 'chuck it in and sort it out' merchants. From an early career in front-wheel drive Peugeots this style has been born of necessity and has served him well in the progression to factory four-wheel drive cars.

Like McRae before him, New Zealand was the venue for his first big win, although it was not a World Championship event that year under the FIA's system of rotating events in and out of the series. With 14 events (whose presence was often due to political expediency to the FIA hierarchy rather than by virtue of being the best rallies in the world) vying for ten slots on the calendar, this was the only way to keep everyone happy. So the 1996 Kiwi win – which followed three successive triumphs for McRae – put Burns firmly on the rally map, although it would be two more years before he scored one that counted, on the 1998 Safari.

Now it's hard to stop him from winning, and the partnership of Englishman Burns and Scottish co-driver Robert Reid is among the most feared in the sport.

Although three seasons at Mitsubishi served as Burns's apprenticeship, it was his return to Subaru that has cast him into the champion's role. Ironically it was again a move triggered by McRae, as Burns filled the seat left vacant when his nemesis departed for Ford. Subaru got the best deal, however, with Burns ending 1999 second to four-time champion Tommi Makinen and running eventual champion Marcus Gronholm all the way to the line in 2000.

STAGE NOTES

Nationality: English
Born: January 17, 1971, Reading, England
Teams: Peugeot 1990–1992, Subaru 1993–1996, Mitsubishi 1996–1998, Subaru 1999–

Career record

First rally: 1988 with Talbot Sunbeam
WRC debut: 1990 Rally GB (Peugeot 309GTI, 28o/a)
WRC starts: 63 **WRC wins:** 9
1998 Safari Rally, Rally GB; 1999 Acropolis Rally, Rally Australia, Rally GB; 2000 Safari, Portugal, Argentina, Rally GB
Stage wins: 172
Honours: 1990–1991 Peugeot Cup Champion, 1992 British National Champion, 1993 British Rally Champion

PETTER SOLBERG

It's only three years since Petter Solberg first tackled a World Championship rally, but he's already set the sport alight and become embroiled in controversy. Norway isn't a country renowned for its rally stars, but Solberg is likely to be the first.

For 2001 Solberg will be a major player for Subaru. The fact that everyone expected him to be a major player for Ford is at the heart of the controversy that surrounded his team swap late last summer.

After only two outings on the WRC in a private Toyota, Ford had seen enough to take Solberg on with the promise of a five-year development programme. It was a dream come true for the (then) 24-year old, taking away the fear that a wrecked car would wipe out his finances and any chance to prove himself.

Solberg lined up for Ford on six events in 1999, but found himself a full member of the team on only his second rally, after Thomas Radstrom fell down the stairs of a hotel in Kenya and broke a leg. The call-up came while Solberg was preparing to tackle a small event at home and he had no time to acclimatise to Kenya, but still finished a remarkable fifth.

He kept the nominated seat for Portugal, but once Radstrom returned in Argentina, the Norwegian reverted to the third car and his original learning curve.

During last season the bubbly Solberg (nicknamed 'Hollywood' because of his boyish good looks) rose through the ranks once again and even got among the pace-setters on several stages. Rival teams knew that Ford had itself a winner for the future – but Subaru discovered that the contract Ford believed it had with Solberg wasn't anything like as watertight as had been claimed.

Faced with the possibility of another three years running as number three to Colin McRae and Carlos Sainz at Ford, or stepping up to be Richard Burns' number two at Subaru, Solberg naturally took the latter option. It was a difficult period for the young driver, but it should not affect his development.

Solberg was Norwegian radio-controlled car champion at 13, stepped up to autocross as soon as possible and won his second race. His older brother Henning, a rally driver of some note, gave him a Ford Escort and he cut his teeth in rallycross and hillclimbing before becoming Norwegian Champion in both in 1995 and 1996.

Again in a Henning hand-me-down, this time a Toyota Celica, Solberg started rallying in 1996. He crashed his first car but stepped aboard an ex-Radstrom Celica to win a third successive hillclimb title in 1997 and take fifth in the Norwegian Rally Championship that same year.

In 1998 he finally became Norwegian Champion and tackled the Swedish and British WRC events, where he caught the eye of Ford boss Malcolm Wilson. Whether or not Wilson wishes he'd not bothered is a moot point for, without a doubt, Solberg is a real 'find' for the championship.

STAGE NOTES

Nationality: Norwegian
Born: November 18, 1974, Spydeberg, Norway
Teams: Toyota 1998, Ford 1999-2000, Subaru 2001

Career record

First rally: 1996 with Toyota Celica
WRC debut: 1998 Swedish (Toyota Celica GT-Four, 16o/a)
WRC starts: 18
WRC wins: 0
Stage wins: 14
Honours: Norwegian Champion 1998

Ford may not love him anymore, but Subaru has welcomed Solberg with open arms.

Waiting in the Wings:
CITROEN
Second Time Lucky

Citroen will make a tentative return to the World Rally Championship during 2001, publicly testing its Xsara T4 on at least four events before a more serious attack next season. The signs are that the T4 will be a winner and a far cry from Citroen's last, pitiful attempt to join the front line some 15 years ago.

The Xsara kit car brought two wins, but the T4 should do even better when it hits the World Championship trail in 2001.

The talk may be of a new Citroen team, but the French outfit has been around for ages. Reports from the 1973 Monte Carlo Rally, the first event to run under the World Championship banner, indicate that Citroen was present then, albeit in privateer form with the unlikely 2CV. It may have been a useful tool in the snow, but...

Move forward two events and you'll find Francisco Romaozinho taking third overall on his native Portugal Rally with a DS21 behind the Renault Alpine A110s of Jean-Luc Therier and Jean-Pierre Nicolas. Two events later and Bob Neyret, Richard Bochnicek and Raymond Ponelle finished second, third and fourth respectively on the Moroccan Rally with a trio of DS23s.

Cast your minds a little further back, to the days before the WRC began, and the records show that the controversial winner of the 1966 Monte Carlo Rally was Pauli Toivonen, father of the late Henri, in a DS21. This was arguably the most well-known event of the pre-WRC era, famous (or more accurately, infamous) because this was the event where the works Minis and the Ford of Roger Clark were excluded from the first four places for a tenuous lighting anomaly.

Having established that Citroen has been around the rally scene since the beginning of time, it is really only recently that the team has had any real success. Before success, however, came abject failure with the BX4TC project that reared its, literally, ugly head in 1986.

After a couple of seasons trying out various prototype vehicles, some based on the Visa and its four-wheel drive 'Mille Pistes' variant, Citroen produced the BX4TC in time for the 1986 Monte Carlo Rally. Compared to the curvaceous lines of its French cousin, Peugeot's dominant 205T16, it looked horrible.

Not only was it ugly, it didn't work either! Philippe Wambergue's car suffered failed suspension on the opening stage of the 1986

FOR THE RECORD

Country of origin: France
Team base: Versailles, France
Date of formation: 1989 (reformed)
WRC debut: Monte Carlo 1986
First WRC win: 1999 Catalunya
WRC wins: 2
Manufacturers titles: 0
Drivers titles: 0

Team specification

Car: Citroen Xsara T4   **Tyres:** Michelin
Sponsors: Automobiles Citroen, Total
Team principal: Guy Frequelin
Designer: Jean-Claude Vaucard

THE VIPS

GUY FREQUELIN

A former driver, Frequelin has hands-on experience of the WRC, desert raids and Le Mans. He joined Citroen in 1990 and masterminded 36 wins from 42 desert raids and both Citroen's WRC event wins.

JEAN-CLAUDE VAUCARD

Vaucard sprung to prominence when he joined Peugeot in 1982 to design the victorious 205T16 and its desert and hillclimb variants. He spent three years on the 905 race project before joining Citroen in 1993.

Monte, its debut rally, and Jean-Claude Andruet's example launched itself off the road a handful of stages later. That both cars had suffered suspension problems on the non-competitive Concentration Run should have served as a warning.

Wambergue's engine failed in Sweden, but Andruet did coax his car home to a respectable sixth, the car's only finish. Citroen stayed at home for a few months and therefore played no part in the fateful Portugal and Corsica events that ultimately led to the scrapping of Group B, but returned, unwisely, for the punishing Acropolis.

Suspension failure (what else?) sidelined Wambergue and Maurice Chomat after the opening stage while Andruet retired two stages later. The fact that the fourth stage was some considerable distance from Athens led many to suspect that Andruet had simply withdrawn, accepting the inevitable rather than waste any more time. Having completed just 65 stages from a possible 270 between its three-car team, the project was cancelled immediately.

Citroen achieved far greater success when it turned its attention to desert raids in the early 1990s. The ZX-based car was essentially the Peugeot 405 Grand Raid rebodied and reflected the new partnership between Citroen and Peugeot in the car market. Among the team's 36 event wins from 42 starts was a staggering run of 28 consecutive wins between January 1994 and November 1997.

Once again, however, rule changes defined Citroen's plans and with the end of the prototype category on desert events, Citroen again turned its attention to conventional rallies.

The ZX model provided useful data, as has the Saxo, but it was the Xsara kit car that catapulted Citroen straight into the thick of things and more than its fair whack of controversy as well.

While the main teams were committed to World Rally Cars and the overall championship, Citroen entered French Championship rounds (which allowed some WRC clashes) with the front-wheel drive Xsara. In a different capacity class to the World Rally Cars, the Xsara enjoyed a lighter weight limit and the chance to use wider tyres. In short, on asphalt, it was more competitive.

Philippe Bugalski won both the Catalunya and Corsica rounds of the 1999 championship and the backlash forced the FIA to change the rules to hobble the lightweight roller-skates.

Citroen, however was already at work on a four-wheel drive WRC version of the Xsara and the T4, as it is known, immediately proved to be quick. Early French Championship events last year, where prototypes were allowed, saw it unbeaten and surely ready for competition. It might have been ready for last season's WRC, but most folk believe that there was an internal conflict between Citroen and Peugeot. After its first test runs the project was inexplicably scrapped and then, just as surprisingly, reinstated. It is believed that the T4 had been held back to give Peugeot at least one full crack at the title before the two teams go head to head. And when that happens, watch out for the fireworks!

Jean-Claude Vaucard created the title-winning Peugeot 205T16. Who'd bet against him at Citroen?

Guy Frequelin was a rally winner himself before joining Citroen as team manager.

WAITING IN THE WINGS

The subject of guest or specialist drivers is likely to be the cause of great debate during 2001. While team managers may dislike the idea, the fact remains that the varied nature of rallies invites the use of drivers whose individual skills allow teams to tailor their squad to a given surface.

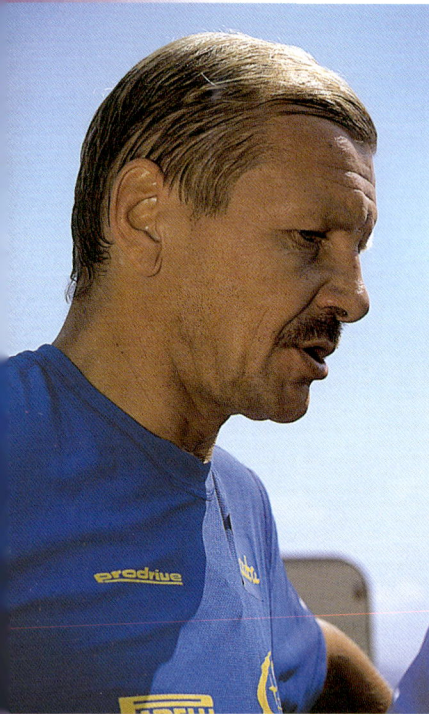

The most successful driver still competing, Juha Kankkunen joins the support cast in 2001.

As the dust settled on the 2000 World Championship, several teams had still not finalised their complete driver line up. Others knew that they had three or four drivers at their disposal. While all drivers are eligible to score points in the drivers' championship, teams can nominate just two for the manufacturers' series points allocation. Inevitably, therefore, drivers will be brought in for limited programmes. These will be for inexperienced drivers' development or because a particular driver can perform better than the regulars on a given surface, asphalt for example.

This policy can also force team managers to rethink their pre-season plans. At the beginning of 2000, Marcus Gronholm was only intended to be a bit-part player at Peugeot. Four events into the year he'd driven himself into a full-time job and, by the end of the year, was king of the hill.

Heading into 2001, the biggest name on the subs' bench is that of **Juha Kankkunen**. Aside from Tommi Makinen he is the sport's only four-time champion and with 23 rally wins to his credit he ranks alongside Carlos Sainz as the most successful driver of all time. His place in the team is always suspect, however, as he has never yet won an asphalt rally and that's quite a weakness for someone of Kankkunen's stature. At 41 the Subaru driver is not completely over the hill but his career has settled into its twilight years and he's not keen to tackle a full season any more.

By contrast, Subaru also has one of the sport's two newest stars on its books. Estonian driver **Markko Martin** is the team's 25-year old newcomer. Along with Petter Solberg he will spend 2001 learning the ropes although Solberg's greater experience will probably see the Norwegian nominated for points on more occasions than Martin. Subaru also used Martinique driver **Simon Jean-Joseph** as an asphalt replacement for Kankkunen in 2000 and it is not beyond possibility that he will be used again in 2001. His name has also been linked to Hyundai's need for an asphalt driver.

The demise of the SEAT team left two drivers out in the cold just when they didn't need to be. Like Kankkunen, 42-year old Didier Auriol has a wealth of experience behind him and the 1994 World Champion will line up with Peugeot in 2001 in a full time seat alongside Marcus Gronholm. His presence in the team gave rise to a bitter row between **Francois Delecour** and Peugeot competition director Corrado Provera that left the mercurial Frenchman holding a P45 instead of contract for 2001 – iit was hard to see what options were left for Delecour...

Sticking with Peugeot, the French team eventually settled on a Gronholm/Delecour combination for most of 2000 but was still able to utilise the asphalt skills of **Gilles Panizzi** to good effect. Wild at times (he was fined in Kenya for punching a fellow competitor) and certainly controversial (he and Delecour nearly came to blows in San Remo amid allegations of illegal reconnaissance by Panizzi) the 25-year old is a natural asphalt driver but nowhere near up to scratch on gravel. This year he will enter the four asphalt events in a factory car plus five gravel events in a semi-works 206WRC from the Grifone team. Also on board is **Harri Rovanpera** who must consider 2001 as a make or break season. The Finn gets seven gravel rallies in a works 206WRC.

The other SEAT refugee is **Toni**

SEAT refugee Toni Gardemeister may have found a berth at Ford in 2001.

Gardemeister. Another 25-year old, the young Finn was a protégé of Kankkunen and very much tipped for the top. Unfortunately SEAT couldn't give him the car to take him there and so in 2001 he will be part of the Ford team. Quite how he'll fit alongside established stars Colin McRae and Carlos Sainz remains to be seen but it's his best opportunity yet to rekindle his career. It is Ford's motorsport director Martin Whitaker who has spoken out most loudly against the use of guest drivers yet it must be remembered that Ford also brought **Piero Liatti** into the squad for San Remo last year to try and keep the team's rival drivers down the order. Liatti, like Jean-Joseph was also linked to Hyundai for 2001.

Citroen's arrival on the scene was still shrouded in a degree of mystery at the time of writing. Outline details of the team's programme with the Xsara T4 and the drivers who will be on board this season were released in early December. Although Auriol's name had been mentioned in early rumours, the drivers most closely associated with the programme are to be team regular **Philippe Bugalski** (who won every one of the car's 'testing' events on the French Championship during 2000) and Spain's **Jesus Puras**. The pair is expected to contest four WRC events (Catalunya, Acropolis, San Remo and Corsica) plus a selection of appropriate national rounds including Britain's Pirelli International Rally. Swedish ex-Ford/Toyota driver **Thomas Radstrom** will stand in for Puras in Greece if there is not sufficient budget for a third car.

Hyundai is another team that needed an asphalt driver to compensate for the lack of sealed surface experience of Kenneth Eriksson and Alister McRae. Puras was the driver regularly tipped for the spot in the closing weeks of last season, but the Citroen deal ended that speculation. Depending on money, Hyundai planned to run three drivers this year but had even considered replacing the 44-year old Swede (the championship's elder statesman) with an all-rounder. In December, however, the Milton Keynes-based team announced that Eriksson would stay with McRae while its asphalt specialist would be Piero Liatti.

The wild cards provide quite a serious bout of intrigue for 2001. Some will play only a minor supporting role while others could blossom into title contenders...

Gilles Panizzi's asphalt pace will again be crucial to Peugeot's title defence.

COURSE DIRECTORY

Rallying stands on the threshold of a Golden Era, a truly global challenge set to rival Formula One for excitement. Television is at the heart of this leap forward and the very fabric of the sport is being tailored to getting the show away from hidden backwaters accessible only to those in the know and into the living rooms of a whole new generation of supporters.

To achieve this brave new world there have been many changes to the events themselves, and while some of the necessary surgery has been painful, it is beginning to pay dividends.

The current calendar remains a blend of both the old and new. Events such as the Monte Carlo Rally have been retained thanks to an abundance of tolerance by the FIA. The innovative approach shown by newcomers such as Australia and Catalunya, however, has demonstrated clearly what can be done with an open mind, a bit of lateral thinking and the determination to blend tough competition into modern commercialism.

There is still work to be done before the FIA achieves its dream of getting rallying onto the television screens – live wherever possible – on the weekends between Grands Prix, but the seeds for such a dream have already been sown.

MONTE CARLO

The Monte Carlo Rally is the most famous event in the world. Everyone wants to win and without it the World Rally Championship would seem hollow. Unfortunately the organisers know this and its organisation leaves a great deal to be desired.

Tommi Makinen threads the needle on his way to victory in 2000.

Ask any schoolboy to name a famous rally and he'll immediately pipe up with the Monte Carlo. This playground for the rich and famous has been attracting the world's greatest and most famous rally drivers for almost 70 years, and will continue to do so for many more.

Yet, instead of being the world's greatest rally and a showpiece opener for the World Championship, all too often the event finds itself in hot water with the FIA over organisational blunders and a trenchant attitude to change. The organisers, the Automobile Club de Monaco, know perfectly well that they have a perceived stranglehold on the FIA over their event's place in the calendar, and there is little doubt that they've got away with things that would have meant other events facing immediate dismissal from the series.

As recently as the 2000 event, the ACM was told by the FIA's safety inspector that one of the stages was too dangerous to go ahead, because spectators had crammed into the stage and had nowhere to run if a car should get out of control. The stage was grudgingly cancelled and the ACM then issued an unbelievable document condemning the decision.

And who, certainly among British rally fans, will ever forget 1966, when the Minis were kicked out? They had won for the previous two years and it was alleged that the organisers couldn't face a third defeat. They dreamed up a weak lighting infringement to exclude the top four cars (three Minis led by Timo Makinen plus the Ford Cortina of Roger Clark) and let Pauli Toivonen's Citroen take the honours. How odd that a French car should benefit...

That said, the Monte remains a classic event, although the shortening of rally formats over recent years has taken out some of the truly great stages (Burzet is probably the biggest 'name' to go in recent years) which were no longer geographically viable. Equally the loss of the Concentration Run was a major step forward and it finally severed the links with the original event.

Getting There

As Monaco doesn't have its own airport it is necessary to fly to Nice. You can then take the bus, train, hire car or (for sheer luxury) the helicopter to the Principality. Hotels in Monaco are expensive and it is easier to stay in France for a fraction of the cost and with better access to the stages.
www.acm.mc/

Star of the Show

In 1985, Ari Vatanen was leading the rally in Peugeot's first full season with the stunning 205 T16 until a rare timing error by his co-driver left the Finn eight minutes adrift. Vatanen set about reeling in four-time Monte winner Walter Rohrl and passed him with seven stages to go. The charismatic Vatanen is now a Euro MP for his native Finland.

The Monte Carlo Rally was created as an excuse for a bit of fun, tempting well-heeled ladies and gentlemen south for the winter. The adventurers started their journeys from towns around Europe before converging on the Principality, where more serious motoring would start. This format remained until 1998 when the needlessly tiring and non-competitive Concentration Run was finally scrapped and the event at last dragged itself into the modern era.

Monaco in January is a pleasant enough spot – which is why people went there in the first place – but up in the mountains it's a different world. Opinions vary as to whether this is an intensely technical event or a complete lottery, but, either way, it's the weather that makes all the difference.

The presence of dry asphalt, ice and snow all together on the same stage is what makes this event special. Certain classic tests such as Sisteron are notoriously prone to this mix of conditions and more than one Monte has been won by an inspired tyre choice. Do you use studded tyres for the ice and snow on the crest and risk having no grip on dry roads for the plunge downhill afterwards, or use unstudded tyres for speed on the dry stuff and hope that the time lost where it's slippery won't be too bad? That's the annual dilemma.

In the 1980s Lancia even tried mid-stage F1-style pit stops to swap tyres after the snow – a bold approach but one now outlawed by servicing restrictions.

The first Monte Carlo Rally was held in 1911. It began on January 21 from half a dozen start points. The 23 crews were allowed to choose their own start time and the only restriction was that they had to arrive in Monaco some time on January 28. Awards were based on the car's speed, the distance travelled, the number of people on board, the comfort level of the car and the state in which it arrived. Henri Rougier, in a Turcat Mery, was declared the winner and pocketed £400 for his troubles. Few people even noticed that the event had taken place.

This all seems a far cry from Tommi Makinen's win in the 2000 event. On that occasion, as is now commonplace, every fraction of a second was hard fought over in front of thousands of screaming partisan fans who gather each year in the mountains and especially on the Col du Turini (arguably the world's most famous rally stage) for their annual party. But then again…

Crowds of spectators and stunning scenery form the backdrop to this historic event.

SWEDEN

Round 2: February 9-11

Sweden in February forms the backdrop for, potentially, one of the most spectacular rallies of the season. Snow and ice make for picture-postcard scenery and the 'back-to-nature' approach of the Swedish people contrasts starkly with the high-octane world of the rally teams.

In theory this event is the only guaranteed snow rally of the season. In practice, the effects of global warming are never more apparent than when the rally circus arrives in Karlstad each February. Although there have been the odd blizzards during the event, recent Swedish rallies have been run more on frozen gravel than on ice covered with thick snow.

Even the traditional stage run on the surface of a frozen lake near Torsby, 100 kilometres north of Karlstad, has become an occasional treat rather than a regular feature of the event. Twice in the past four years the organisers have arranged a stage on the frozen harbour in the centre of Karlstad. While they always insisted that the ice was thick enough to drive a train over, there have been nervous looks on the drivers' faces when they spotted that the surface was covered by an inch of water...

The problem is made worse by the fact that this is a rally where studded tyres are essential. Swedish law demands they be used on the roads at the time of year when the rally takes place, and so there is no way to change to normal gravel tyres for the stages if the surface isn't ideal. And if the surface isn't ideal, then the studs will tear it to shreds. It's a Catch 22 situation.

So far the event has managed to get away with it, although the 1990 rally did have to be cancelled because of the good weather (!) and for similar reasons the 2000 event was looking a little shaky as the teams arrived for the start, but there was deemed to be just enough ice to let the rally run.

The rally may be forced to move further north in the long term to guarantee more predictable conditions or eventually it may have to revert to its original format. From its inception in 1950 until 1964 it was known as the Rally of the Midnight Sun and took place in the summer. The 1965 event was the first to carry the name 'The Swedish Rally' and the first to be run in the winter. Coincidentally both the 1964 and 1965 events were won by Volvo star, Tom Trana.

A glance down the list of former winners reveals one other unique

Snow, snow, quick, quick, snow. This is an event that only the Scandinavians have conquered.

Getting There

Direct flights to Karlstad are not possible, so you must fly via Stockholm or Copenhagen. Karlstad has hire cars but collecting one in Stockholm and making the three-hour drive is another option. Hotels are reasonably plentiful but can be expensive and are booked up very quickly. www.swerally.se/

Marcus Gronholm's first WRC win came on last year's Swedish Rally.

fact about this event. No one from outside the Baltic countries has ever won it! Every other event in the series has been won by Europeans and Scandinavians alike, but not this one. The closest is Carlos Sainz, finishing second on every event between 1996–1999, never more than a minute behind the leader. Nevertheless, outright victory continues to elude him.

Another second-place man was Colin McRae who, in 1992, served notice to the world of what was about to come.

The Swedish Rally requires a different style of driving from anywhere else. On the other 13 events of the series drivers will use familiar gravel or asphalt tyres with predictable handling characteristics. Tyres used in Sweden are unlike any other. They are narrow, almost bicycle-like by comparison, and fitted with longer studs than those permitted on the Monte Carlo Rally.

Cars take on an odd appearance in Sweden because the spindly wheels look out of place on cars with wide wheel arches. They appear to stand much taller and the deflection in the tyre shape is often quite readily apparent. Nevertheless they offer staggering amounts of grip on roads where spectators sometimes can barely stand upright and the Swedish Rally is by no means the slowest event in the championship.

Driving technique is different as well. Drivers try to follow racing lines on asphalt and, despite flinging the tail of their cars out at odd angles, always try to stay away from the banks on gravel. If the Swedish Rally manages to get snow then there will be snow banks at the edge of the ploughed roads. The top crews bounce their cars off these to keep themselves on the road while driving at speeds far above those that would seem prudent in the conditions.

The Swedish Rally is one of the oldest in the championship, but it is not one where time stands still. The weather may determine many of the things that can or can't be done, but the organisers are forward thinking and willing to experiment with fresh ideas. Because of its specialist nature, however, it is still not a good form guide to the season and the drivers will have to wait a couple more events before the results start to show any true indication of who's seriously on the title trail.

Star of the Show

Kenneth Eriksson is the current top Swede but the Swedish Rally belongs to Stig Blomqvist. The veteran driver can look back on a record five wins in his home event since the World Championship was created. He won with Saab (1973, 1977 and 1979) before taking two more wins for Audi in 1982 and his title-winning year of 1984.

PORTUGAL

Portugal is generally regarded as the first 'proper' rally of the year as the early events of the season have an element of the lottery about them. Here is where the form guide can be opened and where the first ideas about which teams and drivers are likely to lift the crown by the end of the season can be had.

During the late 1970s and early 1980s Portugal was a nightmare event. Manic crowds of rally fans with little or no regard for their own safety were allowed to do as they pleased by police and marshals who stood by and watched. Injured spectators were considered an acceptable risk until a car spun into the crowd, killing three and injuring ten times that number, in 1986. The incident was captured on film and when the horrific scenes were shown on news bulletins around the world it provided a major jolt to the organisers.

That fatal accident, when Joaquim Santos' Ford RS200 shot into the uncontrolled crowd in the walled town of Sintra, sparked a drivers' revolt. They were no longer prepared to ignore

Portuguese spectators pack the hillsides. Arrive early to avoid disappointment!

the crowd. After a meeting in the Estoril Rally HQ, the leading crews defied their team managers and withdrew from the rally

The spring of 1986 was a dark time for the sport. The Group B cars, of which Ford's RS200 was just one of many, were no longer controllable even by the top drivers. It had been widely expected that the World Championship that year would be won by Finnish ace Henri Toivonen. Two events after Portugal he was dead, killed instantly along with his co-driver Sergio Cresto after his Lancia plunged off the road in a Corsican fireball. Group B was cancelled by the FIA from the end of the season (Audi withdrew immediately, claiming that if the cars were dangerous then they should be scrapped straight away and not later) and new formulae were immediately placed on the agenda.

From this traumatic period (Toivonen was rallying's equivalent of Ayrton Senna at that time and so this was equally as hard a blow to take) a brave new world for cars and events emerged.

Although the rally continued to be based at Estoril, along the coast from Lisbon, concentrations of stages in confined areas were phased out to prevent large crowds gathering in one place. Eventually the rally abandoned Estoril as the demands for more compact routes grew more forceful.

The southern asphalt stages were also abandoned and the rally briefly based itself at the coastal resort of Figueira da Foz (1995–1997) before moving into the historic city of Porto. The rally has now found its true

Getting There

Flights to Porto are simple but if they get booked up it's no drama to fly to Lisbon and drive. Rally HQ is out of town so you'll need a car, but make sure you're well insured against the local drivers. www.tap-rallyedeportugal.pt/

Portugal offers some spectacular viewing as cars power through the countryside.

home, one where the enthusiastic tourist board can promote its country. The event has long been backed by, primarily, TAP (Portugal's national airline being on board right from the start in 1967) and the port wine industry, and visitors are treated to a constant stream of promotional events that few other rallies care to attempt to match.

Images of Portugal centre on the famous big jump at Fafe, where the fans gather to judge the height and distance competition and signal their approval with raucous cheers. For the record the 2000 winner was Armin Schwarz's Skoda.

After Markku Alen had clinched his fifth event win in 1987, his Lancia team mate Miki Biasion rattled off a hat-trick of victories from 1988–1990. The last of the three marked an astonishing result for Lancia, the Italians taking the top five places overall and the top three in Group N – a record that none has yet come close to matching. It should be remembered, however, that Lancia was the dominant team throughout the second half of the 1980s.

The early part of that decade featured the four-wheel drive revolution, led by Audi and quickly embraced by all the major players. While Michele Mouton's 1982 success for the German team was not her first World Championship rally win, it was one of three that year that would see her in a head-to-head battle with Walter Rohrl for the championship crown. Although Rohrl eventually emerged as the winner, Mouton did wonders for the image of women in motorsport, even though the FIA still needed another eight years to create a Ladies Cup!

Recent seasons have included even greater steps forward for safety and organisation, along with Portugal being one of the few events to enjoy extensive live television coverage, while head-to-head superspecial stages were a popular Portuguese innovation. The event also witnessed the closest finish ever when, in 1998, Colin McRae's ailing Subaru edged out Carlos Sainz's Toyota by just 2.1 seconds. In 2000, Richard Burns's victory made him the first Englishman ever to lead the World Championship while, further back and relatively unnoticed, America driver John Buffum (who won more international events than anyone in the sport) finally hung up his helmet.

Star of the Show

The driver most synonymous with Portugal Rally victories is Markku Alen. Although Finnish he may as well have been Italian, because his successes were mainly at the wheel of a Fiat/Lancia group machine. Of his five Portugal wins four (1975, '77, '78 and '81) were in Fiats before he won for Lancia in 1987. Despite 20 rally victories, Alen never won the title.

CATALUNYA

The final-day battle between Colin McRae, Richard Burns and Carlos Sainz to decide the winner of the 2000 Catalunya Rally had people on the edge of their seats. This is one of the most emotive events of the year, but not always for obvious reasons...

Whoever designed this motorway bridge had no idea that it would become a grandstand.

It was a case of lucky 13 for Spain when, after 12 previous events, the Catalunya-Costa Brava Rally joined the World Rally Championship in 1991. The rally in those days was run in November and it stayed that way until 1997, when the date was switched to spring.

That first event could have been the scene of a major celebration, for local hero Carlos Sainz was perfectly poised to clinch the World Championship. The man from Madrid, ironically, had never won his home event, but this wasn't to be the occasion to break his duck. As he lined up to leave the seafront parc ferme in Lloret de Mar for the second day, his Toyota refused to start and, in disbelief, he had no choice but to walk away. Cruelly, having been so close to winning his second title in front of his adoring fans, Sainz could finish only third on the final event of the year and the title went to Juha Kankkunen instead.

Although Sainz slipped up, Toyota went on to win the event despite a dramatic final day. Team mechanics had to perform a lightning-quick gearbox change on rally leader Armin Schwarz's car in the main street of the town before he could set off for the stages, and then the German rolled the car and lost a further minute. Schwarz, however, was far enough ahead for these incidents not to matter and the first WRC Catalunya Rally went down in history as Schwarz's only premier league victory.

Sainz got his revenge the following season, leading from start to finish to become the first Spanish winner for eight seasons. It wasn't quite a title-decider, but Sainz went on to record the double and take the second of his two world crowns.

The event had been a mixture of gravel and asphalt, but in 1993, in line with more and more events, it was changed to a single surface. Asphalt was the chosen option and Ford's Francois Delecour took the first sealed surface Catalunya Rally. Third place racked up Kankkunen's fourth World Championship title, adding to Toyota's first Manufacturers' crown gained two events earlier.

Star of the Show

Carlos Sainz is a hero in Spain. Everywhere he goes he is cheered to the echo and never more than during the Catalunya Rally – although he was never a winner before the event's promotion to the WRC, he has since won twice (in 1992 and '95) and has been frequently denied by the cruellest luck. Not that the fans care!

This is one of the cheapest events to visit thanks to budget flights to Barcelona or Girona and lots of cheap accommodation in Lloret de Mar. It's also one of the easiest rallies to follow, but the roads do get busy. www.rallyecatalunya.com/

Spain's giant car manufacturer, SEAT, used the non-championship 1994 event to relaunch its international rally programme and the Barcelona-based team has been a major player ever since.

The Catalunya Rally has been a prime mover in rally organisation. The ever-present problem of spectator control in the 'Latin' nations was efficiently dealt with and other events have been able to learn from Spain's example. Many times the event has won awards for its organisational standards and yet, through no fault of its own, has been involved in great controversy over the years.

In 1995 the headlines simply dropped out of the skies! First Tommi Makinen crashed out of the event and his Mitsubishi slid straight into the side of a misparked ambulance. Then there was the Subaru team orders drama...

With the team holding 1-2 at the end of the penultimate day, team boss David Richards ordered that Sainz and Colin McRae should now hold station to maximise the team's points haul and virtually assure Subaru of its first Manufacturers' Championship. The problem was that McRae kept the hammer down and blasted past Sainz into the lead. McRae refused to slow down and emerged from the stages in the lead. A furious row in the main street erupted but the team held sway and McRae checked into the final control late to hand the win back to Sainz. It is an issue that still rankles between them to this day.

Even that was not enough for this event. A tip-off had alerted officials to a potential problem with the turbos on the three Toyotas. Didier Auriol's car was found to be at fault and

was promptly excluded. Subsequent examination of the others revealed an ingenious construction that had allowed all three cars to bypass the FIA-imposed air restrictors and gain extra power. A few weeks later the FIA threw Toyota out of the championship and imposed a further year's ban – the heaviest penalty yet given out by the sport's ruling body, but one that made everyone sit up and take notice.

Since then the biggest row came when Philippe Bugalski won for Citroen in 1999, the first time a two-wheel drive car had won a qualifying round for ten years. It just goes to show that when you come to Spain, anything can happen.

Spanish fans watch safely as Alister McRae powers past.

No rain on this Spanish plain. A typical Catalunya backdrop.

ARGENTINA

Round 5: May 4-6

Rallying has enjoyed a rich history in Argentina and the travelling circus always enjoys a warm welcome in the land of the Gaucho. It's among the fastest events in the series, and provides spectacular viewing for the spectators.

Right from the start, 20 years ago, there was a World Championship event in Argentina. The 1980 event was known as the Codasur Rally and was won by that season's World Champion, Walter Rohrl, driving a Fiat 131. Since then the event has gone through changes of both name and start venue, but it remains one of those events that people enjoy going to, even though getting to Cordoba – its present base – involves one of the most complicated journeys of the season.

Like the Monte Carlo Rally, Argentina's prime event began with a long-winded format where crews started from four cities in different South American countries; Argentina, Brazil, Paraguay and Uruguay. Once the Concentration Run was over the rally was then based in the northern town of Tucuman, with stages run in some pretty remote areas.

Getting There

This is one of the toughest events of the year to get to. You can either fly to Buenos Aires, change airports, and then fly to Cordoba, or fly via Sao Paolo in Brazil. Flights are expensive, hire cars extortionate, but you'll definitely be made welcome! www.rallyarg.com.ar/

In 1980 Mercedes entered a four-car team of 500SLCs although only one car survived, driven by Hannu Mikkola into second place, some 16 minutes adrift of the winner. Andrew Cowan (now boss at Mitsubishi) suffered head gasket failure, while broken driveshafts saw off Bjorn Waldegard and the emerging local hero, Jorge Recalde.

Aside from Juan Manuel Fangio's appearance as a Mercedes party guest, the event also involved F1 star Carlos Reutemann, taking time out from the busy racing season to finish third in what could best be described as a marathon event. At almost 1,200kms of competitive mileage and at up to 3,700 metres above sea level, this was the highest WRC event ever. Argentina also holds the all-time stage record of 189kph and the fastest overall average speed.

The rally was put on hold in 1982 because of the Falklands conflict. In 1983 the event had moved to Bariloche, but although it made one more trip back to Tucuman, the event has now settled in Cordoba. Ironically, while the administrative centre is in this major city, the teams stay a few kilometres down the road at Villa Carlos Paz. This holiday resort has more

Time to freshen up! There are lots of water splashes in Argentina.

Star of the Show

South America has a fine stock of local drivers, but only two have ever made a serious impact on the World Championship. Jorge Recalde remains the only Argentine driver ever to take a WRC win and that was inevitably in his home event in 1988. He has since ventured onto the Group N World Championship but has been overshadowed by Uruguay's four-time champion, Gustavo Trelles.

hotels in a smaller area and is therefore a more attractive proposition.

The Argentine Rally was at the centre of a dramatic moment in Ari Vatanen's life. The Finnish legend was chasing the 1985 World Championship when he rolled his Peugeot 205T16 at high speed. The car was completely destroyed and the crew were lucky to escape with their lives. Co-driver Terry Harryman broke his neck, while Vatanen was hospitalised with severe leg injuries and mental scars that took over a year to heal. Both men recovered, but it is a period described with astonishing candour in Vatanen's autobiography, *Every Second Counts*.

Illness has twice affected this event. In 1993 co-driver Juha Piironen was struck down with a brain haemorrhage just before the start. Mitsubishi 'loaned' Nicky Grist to Toyota and the instant new pairing of Grist and Juha Kankkunen went on to record Toyota's 30th WRC victory.

In the following year Didier Auriol beat Carlos Sainz by six seconds, the closest finish in six years, while there was great emotion when Vatanen took third.

Tommi Makinen has won this event three times (1996–1998) although the first of his three wins was overshadowed by the antics of reigning world champion Colin McRae. He crashed twice before retiring and was reported for speeding in a service area. The FIA summoned him to Paris (in the middle of the recce for the next event) and fined him $75,000 for the service area offence, while his team manager threatened him with the sack if he didn't raise his standards. Ironically it was his co-driver, Derek Ringer, who was eventually kicked out of the team to be replaced by … Nicky Grist.

Makinen's hat-trick of wins coincided with the first three years of his tenure as quadruple World Champion. He seemed able to win as he liked while the others simply fought for second. And how they fought! In 1998 Sainz edged out Kankkunen by just 0.7s and the rival crews worked out that the gap equated to a mere 20 metres. Rallying had become an incredibly close affair.

In 1999 Kankkunen gained revenge and won the event outright, although in controversial circumstances. Subaru team mate Richard Burns expected Kankkunen to hold station behind him, according to the team's instructions, but the Finn stole the win on the final stage. Burns hit back with a crushing victory in 2000.

Fast stages, close finishes, the best steaks in the world and some of the prettiest girls you could wish to find. Argentina has got the lot …

CYPRUS

Round 6: June 1–3

The Cyprus Rally was catapulted into the World Rally Championship at very short notice during 2000. As a long-time leading round of the European series it now has the chance to establish itself at the top level. There is some opposition to its presence, however, and so it will have to work hard to stay on the calendar.

The Cyprus Rally takes crews high into the Troodos mountains.

When Cyprus first began running rallies they were more a survival of the fittest with the last man standing often declared the winner. Some might claim that nothing has changed as the rough nature of the roads, coupled with the searing heat (at least during its September date) and very slow speeds continue to make this an especially tough challenge.

For most crews who ventured to the island event for the first time in 2000, after the rally had been thrown in at the deep end as a last-minute replacement for the financially challenged China Rally, everything was a new experience. However, the newest event in the World Championship has a richer history than some may expect.

As cars became more sophisticated and reliable, the early Cyprus events – little more than a cross between a race and a reliability trial – were no longer acceptable to the local drivers. In 1970, therefore, the Cyprus AA approached Rothmans for advice on how to make things a bit more professional and the Cyprus Rally was born. Hannu Mikkola was a competitor on the first Cyprus Rally, but even the great man himself was beaten by mechanical failure when the engine of his Ford Escort let go. Instead of Mikkola (with three 1000 Lakes rallies and a World Cup Rally already on his win list even before the World Championship was created) taking the honours, the first Cyprus Rally was won by a Fiat 125 crammed with Victor Zachariades, Loris Ellinas and Roger Fisher. Yes, a three-man crew!

The local champion, Chris Kirmitsis, took the following year's event and it was not until 1972 before the first star name climbed to the top step of the podium. That man was Stig Blomqvist and his Saab 96 had annihilated the opposition.

The future of the event suddenly looked shaky for in 1974 the Turks annexed the northern part of the island. Even to this day United Nations peacekeepers continue to keep the two factions apart, although Cyprus cannot be considered a war zone.

Rallying resumed in 1976 and the event was won by Shekhar Mehta, now the FIA Rallies Commission president, and Yvonne Pratt, whose Datsun beat Antonio Zanini's SEAT. The winning duo is now better known as Mr and Mrs Mehta.

Salvador Canellas took second again for

SEAT the following year, but in 1978 the event, now promoted to coefficient 3 of the European Championship (just one step from the top level), was won by the late Roger Clark.

Rothmans became title sponsor in 1979 and from then on the event had the feel of a slightly detuned World Championship event. The cigarette giant brought in a fresh level of professionalism and ensured that more and more people got to know about this little gem of an event.

Rothmans also backed its sponsorship by bringing its own contracted drivers to the event to raise the standard. Ari Vatanen and co-driver David Richards won for the Rothmans team in 1980 and the following season Clark became the first driver to take two wins, a record that stood for 14 years. While another local driver, Vahan Terzian, won the following year, second place was enough to clinch the European title for Jochi Kleint.

By 1982 the event had been promoted to the top level in Europe. The Euro series was a long drawn out affair, often won long before the

finish by the richest driver and with little or no outside interest. In the island's first year at the top, however, Tony Fassina won both the event and the title after the Rothmans star invitee, Jimmy McRae, had had an early retirement. By now many drivers and their families were discovering that Cyprus in September offered an ideal chance for a late summer holiday. This will be the case in 2001, as the June date should see many holidaymakers among the spectators.

In the ensuing seasons drivers such as Fabrizio Tabaton and Armin Schwarz clinched the European crown with victory in Cyprus, while Toyota used the event to test its new Celica GT-Four in 1988, winning with Bjorn Waldegard. Alex Fiorio ended Clark's tenure as the only man to win twice when he went one better with a hat-trick of wins for the Astra team from 1992–1994.

The event has moved base from the centrally-based capital, Nicosia, to the southern coastal resort of Limassol to cope with the demands for hotel beds by the major teams. The twisty stages are not to everyone's liking, but the organisation proved well above average. Cyprus has already set standards that others will do well to match.

Twisty stages make this one of the slowest events of the year.

ACROPOLIS

Round 7: June 15-17

Rock-strewn roads and high temperatures are the hallmarks of this Greek classic. It's not as fast as the Safari, nor as much of a lottery, but the Acropolis is still a matter of survival for even the top teams.

One of the toughest events in the championship, the Acropolis is also one of the oldest, heading into its 48th year in 2001. Nevertheless, despite its age, getting a car to the finish has not become any easier, as last year's event proved all too clearly. Ford took an orchestrated 1-2 for Colin McRae and Carlos Sainz respectively, but the rest of the field were left in tatters.

The best-prepared cars in the world, driven by the best drivers the teams could muster, simply failed to stay the course. Only Juha Kankkunen's Subaru and Armin Schwarz's Skoda were still there at the finish along with the Fords. The rest were broken-down victims of the punishing gravel roads.

The Acropolis Rally owes its origins to the 1952 Rally ELPA, the first to be organised in Greece since the war. That event was won by

You can find water in Greece, but it's a rare sight at rallytime!

Johnny Pezmazoglou, but it was Nic Papamichael's Jaguar XK120 one year later which took the honours as the first winner of the Acropolis Rally as we know it.

Right from the start the event got under way from beneath the Acropolis in the heart of Athens. This tradition is all very well, but it must be said that maintaining it has caused more problems than necessary. With the current desire for events to return to a single HQ town each night you need only ask anyone who has attempted to drive in Athens how sensible a plan that would be!

Without a doubt the traffic contributed to Kenneth Eriksson's not finishing higher than seventh in 1991. A road accident immediately after the start ramp cost him seven minutes of road penalties while the battered Mitsubishi Galant (on its World rally debut) was patched up. The Swede went on to set 30 fastest times, but was never going to get close enough to challenge eventual winner Juha Kankkunen – who set only two...

In recent years the event has moved to a variety of locations in a quest to find the perfect host while still trying to find a way to get the cars to Athens for the traditional start ceremony. The event, by necessity, has taken on a kind of 'gypsy' mentality that will remain until the organisers finally break with tradition.

The event went international in 1956 when the Mercedes 300SL driven by Walter Schock took the honours, and three years later Wolfgang Levy's Auto Union 1000 scored the first victory on a European Championship-qualifying Acropolis.

Unlike many events, the Greek rally has

Kenneth Eriksson kicks up the stones in 2000.

survived with only one non-start in its history. That came in 1974 when the Turkish invasion of Cyprus caused political turmoil in the region.

The 1973 season included the birth of the World Rally Championship (although the international series that preceded it bore a striking similarity in its calendar) and victory in Greece fell to the Alpine Renault A110 driven by French ace, Jean-Luc Therier.

Therier had won once before, in 1969, and already the winners list read like a 'Who's Who' of rallying, including Erik Carlsson, Eugen Bohringer, Tom Trana, Bengt Soderstrom, Paddy Hopkirk, Roger Clark, Pauli Toivonen (father of the late Henri) and Toyota boss Ove Andersson.

After the 1974 hiatus, Walter Rohrl was the first of the new generation of drivers to win the event as part of their quest for the World Rally Championship. In 1973, however, it was just a competition for manufacturers and not until 1979 was a drivers' series added.

Rohrl and Bjorn Waldegard each won two of the next five events with Harry Kallstrom taking the other before Ari Vatanen bagged a brace in 1980 and 1981. This latter was in his title-winning season when he became the only driver in a private team to take the crown.

Almost a decade later Carlos Sainz won his first World Rally and went on to lift the 1990 title, the first for a Toyota driver. Other significant moments in the event's history include Lancia star Didier Auriol's first gravel win, the first for Subaru in Europe and the first for the Impreza anywhere.

The roughness of the event caused tyre companies to evolve new technology and at the

end of the 1980s Michelin had launched the now ubiquitous 'mousse' system that fills the space as air escapes from the tyre after a puncture. On the 1989 event several fastest stage times were taken by cars with punctures, thanks to this system, and arch-rivals Pirelli soon followed suit.

Star of the Show

On this event in 1975 a German named Walter Rohrl took his first World Championship win, driving an Opel Ascona. He was already European Champion but by the time he'd added the 1978 (Fiat) and 1983 (Lancia) events to his tally he'd won the title twice. The mercurial Rohrl was rallying's equivalent of Michael Schumacher.

Dust clouds, enthusiastic fans and vague maps. That's the Acropolis for you.

SAFARI
Round 8: July 20-22

If the Monte Carlo Rally is the glamour event of the World Rally Championship then the Safari is the one that every manufacturer wants to crack, just to prove how tough their cars are. It may have changed over the years, but it's still a classic.

They call the Safari the 'World's Toughest Rally' and they're not kidding! Some of the current competitive sections (this event still can't quite bring itself to call them special stages) are longer than a whole day's action in Europe and the speeds are higher than on many other events.

It's also unique in that the Safari is the only rally not to run on closed roads. Therefore, aside from the usual everyday hazards facing any rally driver, the Safari chucks in local traffic, errant pedestrians and of course any number of wild animals wandering across the road without warning.

To cope with this, each of the top crews will have a helicopter 'spotter' flying just ahead of him on the road with the airborne 'eyes' in constant radio contact to warn of anything amiss ahead. It all adds to the cost of this event, one that's already higher than any other because of the need to build uniquely strong cars that are too heavy to be used anywhere else.

The first automobile arrived in Kenya in 1903, but it was nearly 30 years before you could actually drive between major cities such as Nairobi and Mombasa, let alone between countries in East Africa. Over the next 20 years, however, motoring and motorsport grew in popularity. A competitions committee was created and an event, running from Dar es Salaam in Tanganyika to Nairobi via the Ugandan capital of Entebbe, was discussed. The rally never actually came to fruition thanks to a period of political fragility, but by the spring of 1952 things were changing. Eric Cecil, one of the original committee members, had the idea of a rally around Lake Victoria using the three countries.

Queen Elizabeth's accession to the throne in 1953 proved the catalyst and the rally was to be part of the celebrations. Hence the Coronation Safari Rally was created and a legend was born. It was a pretty basic event with 56 starters and only 16 finishers inside the time limit. No outright winner was declared.

The event quickly grew in popularity with the pairing of Vic Preston Sr and Dr D.P. Marwaha winning the next two events in a VW Beetle.

Cecil, known as 'the father of the Safari' resigned from the committee in order to compete and he went on to win the event in 1956. Perhaps coincidentally, on that same event, Dutch driver Maurice Gatsonides (he of the infamous Gatso speed camera) promised to tell his friends about his adventures when he

Safari sunrise and the tell-tale lights of an approaching car.

Getting There

Flights to Nairobi are not as plentiful these days, but they are not expensive. Why not combine the event with a Safari holiday and get better value for money? Kenya is good to explore, but play it safe in towns.
www.safarirally.co.ke/

Shekhar Mehta was the king of the Safari in the late 1970s with four successive wins from 1979–1982 adding to his 1973 win. All were at the wheel of Datsuns (or by 1982, Nissan) and his four-in-a-row record stood for 16 years before Tommi Makinen equalled it in Finland. Today Mehta is the well-respected president of the FIA Rallies Commission.

got home. The following year the FIA included the Safari on its international calendar and shifted it to what would become a traditional Easter slot.

As Easter is a moveable feast in the religious calendar, the conditions faced by the event became notoriously unpredictable and gave rise to its growing reputation for toughness. Some years would be bone dry and others would fall right in the middle of the region's rainy season.

By the early 1960s the number of overseas crews was growing with each event and factory teams were also seen to be taking an interest. Amid a massive rainstorm the 1963 rally looked to be going Eric Carlsson's way, but, despite a massive lead, he was forced out after hitting an animal.

As the years progressed the question on most people's lips was, 'When is an overseas driver going to win?' By the time the event was promoted to the International Rally Championship for Makes (the 12-round fore-runner of the World Rally Championship) in 1970 the question remained unanswered. East African drivers dominated the results in a variety of cars, most notably the Peugeot 404 and, in 1964, a Ford Cortina GT driven by Peter Hughes, the eventual Clerk of the Course.

Eventually the dam was breached and in 1972 Hannu Mikkola scored an historic first win for the visitors, driving a Ford Escort that now sits in the Ford rally team's new Cumbrian headquarters as part of a Safari Rally display.

In the following year Shekhar Mehta took the first of what would be five wins and in 1974 Joginder Singh gave Mitsubishi (under the Colt banner) its first World rally success. Singh (known as 'the Flying Sikh') would win one more event, but aside from Mehta's record-run between 1979–1982, that was it for the local crews and the Europeans took over.

The event has been shortened, technology has turned it into a sprint and even first-time drivers (Juha Kankkunen and Tommi Makinen) have proved it can be beaten. Nevertheless it still remains a tough nut to crack.

Richard Burns proved a dominant winner in 2000.

African fans turn out in their thousands to watch the fun.

FINLAND

The Safari Rally may epitomise the adventurous origins of rallying, but for sheer exhilaration nothing can match the Finnish round of the series. Pin-point accuracy and unmatched bravery are the key elements for a driver hoping to win this one.

Officially this event is called Neste Rally Finland, but you'll be hard pushed to find anyone who doesn't refer to it by its old name: the 1,000 Lakes Rally. The arrival of a contractually named sponsor, Neste, and a major reworking of the organisational structure of Finnish motorsport enforced the name change, but the character of the event remains the same.

The rally of 1,000 jumps might be a more accurate title. If photographers can't get one of Finland's lakes in the background of the shot then you can bet that the cars are so far off the ground that the driver ought to be asked for his pilot's licence.

The smooth gravel surface belies the treachery of this event, for very few can master the subtleties of grip and traction offered by the switchback roads of central Finland.

Unusually this is a rally that has never switched around its headquarters and has been based in the university town of Jyvaskyla since its inception in 1951. The route has changed quite radically, however, and instead of the broad loop north to Rovaniemi on the edge of the Arctic Circle, the event now follows the modern cloverleaf format. Some of the classic stages have been lost, either by the need to make the event more compact or by having to cut the risk factor as speeds increased. Nevertheless this is still an event at the spiritual heart of rallying.

The fact that Finland still has a large number of its public roads deep in the forests mean that asphalt surfaces are not as plentiful as in other European countries. Driving speeds in Finland are very low and the Finnish police enforce the law with oppressive rigidity. This has meant that the local drivers, for whom the roads are a way of life, have an inbuilt sense of the achievable while the visitors never fully understand what they are doing.

The outcome of this is that, with the exception of Carlos Sainz (Toyota, 1990) and Didier Auriol (Lancia, 1992), this is another of those events where the Scandinavian drivers have ruled the roost.

Eric Carlsson's 1957 win was the first on the list for what could be described as a 'name' driver before Rauno Aaltonen won for Mercedes in

They called it the 1,000 Lakes Rally. Here is just one of them.

Getting There

Getting to Helsinki is easy but flying on to Jyvaskyla can be tricky because seats go quickly. A hire car can save the day but driving in Finland is slow. Still, there's time to enjoy the scenery. Local hotels are basic but comfortable.

www.akkry.fi/nesterallyfinland/

1961. Citroen's Pauli Toivonen added his name to the winners' roll of honour the following year before current rally director Simo Lampinen took the first of his two wins for Saab in 1963 and 1964.

The mighty Mini, with its most burly occupant, Timo Makinen, was a hat-trick winner over the next three events before Hannu Mikkola took the first of what would be an all-time record of eight wins over the next 15 years. Mikkola, doyen of Finnish drivers, took a hat-trick between 1968–1970, and back-to-back wins in 1974–1975 and 1982–1983. The latter success was in an Audi Quattro while the hat-trick was at the wheel of a Ford Escort. Ford supplied the car for 1974, but the 1975 win was the first for the newly-formed Toyota Team Europe.

Markku Alen is Mikkola's closest rival with six wins, but Tommi Makinen ('No relation,' says Timo. 'I think!') outran them both with five in a row to show his total domination of the event between 1994–1998, the latter being the 100th win for a Japanese car.

The event statistics just roll out. In the 1992 event Lancia won a sixth consecutive (and final) world title, while in 1993 Mikkola entered his final rally of an illustrious career spanning almost three decades. Toyota's second consecutive Manufacturers' title was confirmed in 1994, the same year that Makinen won his first World Rally in a Ford Escort Cosworth.

Jarmo Kytolehto's third place in 1996, ahead of all the factory Fords, was a key moment in M-Sport's ultimately successful bid to land the contract to run the Ford team. The following year marked the return of the disgraced Toyota team, giving the Corolla WRC its championship debut in the hands of current Peugeot star, Marcus Gronholm.

SEAT entered front-line competition with the Cordoba WRC at this event in 1998 and a year later Kankkunen confirmed his place as the championship's most successful driver with his 23rd World Rally win.

Statistics, however, are but a part of the Finnish Rally's success story. The Finns have dominated rallying for so long that this is the sport's 'home' event. Other countries may be more passionate about motorsport in general, but nowhere are the sport's stars feted more than here among the pine trees and lakes.

There are so many jumps on the event that you need a pilot's licence.

Star of the Show

Finland is rallying's spiritual home and so 'stars' are ten a penny. Tommi Makinen, however, is only man to win this event five times in a row, starting with his first WRC event success in 1994. His first win was with Ford, the rest with Mitsubishi, and it's a record that will take some beating.

NEW ZEALAND

The New Zealand Rally has entered the 21st century with a fresh face and a well-received change of attitude. The furthest event for most of the teams, New Zealand has had to work hard to hold its place in the championship.

Of all the current rounds, the Rally of New Zealand has had the most chequered past. Simply by being so far away for the bulk of the competing teams, the Kiwis have to offer the very best organisation and route when the crews arrive, jet-lagged and weary, after around 24 hours in the air. That the event hasn't always delivered explains why, at times, it has been little more than an occasional player. As late as 1998 there were calls for New Zealand to be dropped from the calendar.

The wave of complaints in 1998 served as a wake-up call. For 1999 the event was moved into the heart of Auckland and based at the awesome Sky Tower, the tallest building in the Southern Hemisphere. The showpiece structure, coupled with a rash of upmarket shops and restaurants that sprung up in the wake of Team New Zealand's successful America's Cup campaign, opened people's eyes to Auckland itself. The organisers picked up on the buzz and when the teams arrived for the 2000 event, the rally's 30th anniversary, it was with more enthusiasm than had been seen for some time.

If attitudes and location had managed to kill off this event it would have been a shame, for New Zealand offers some of the best 'drivers' stages of the championship. They are smooth, fast and flowing and are almost universally enjoyed. Winter in New Zealand has made this event pretty tricky, however, and so it's no piece of cake for the successful crew.

The modern New Zealand Rally is a far cry from the original Shell Silver Fern of 1969. That event was so new in concept that crews were wondering why they had to pack crash helmets! It was won by Grady Thomson, driving a powerful Holden Monaro V8, who easily outpaced his 32 rivals.

A Ford Anglia nearly won the 1970 event, but a massive navigational blunder by Mike Marshall let Paul Adams in for a win in his BMW 2002. Andrew Cowan, now the Mitsubishi boss, made the trip in 1971, but his Mini was blighted with mechanical problems and the Cortina GT of Aussie driver Bruce Hodgson went on to win. Cowan swapped from his intended Morris Marina back to the Mini just before the start of the 1972 event, and he went on to record a famous victory.

In those early years the event was run under the banner of the Heatway International Rally

Twisting roads lined with pampas grasses are a feature of the event.

The coast roads provide a stunning backdrop for Rally New Zealand.

and was not confined, as it is now, to the North Island roads. The 1973 event was an inter-island affair, running for eight days and over 2,800kms of stages. International ace, Hannu Mikkola, won the event, not surprisingly the longest-ever NZ rally, for Ford, ahead of Marshall. The 1974 event was cancelled because of the oil crisis and when it resumed in 1975 Marshall finally got the win he'd been chasing. The Millen brothers fought for second place, Steve getting the drop on Rod at the finish.

In 1976, Cowan defied snow and ice in the South Island to take a second win, this time in a Hillman Avenger, before Fulvio Bacchelli edged out Ari Vatanen in a classic 1977 battle between Fiat and Ford.

The 1978 event was dumped from the World Championship, but was another British success, this time for Russell Brookes. The event was back in favour for 1979 when Mikkola romped home ahead of Timo Salonen's Datsun before the latter was excluded when his team refused to let scrutineers strip the engine after the event. He gained his revenge the following year!

Local drivers had it their own way in 1981 when the event again found itself out of favour. Jim Donald won this one while many were impressed by the speed of a young newcomer named Peter Bourne. Eventually, and now nicknamed 'Possum', Bourne became New Zealand's top driver and is currently a multiple Australian Champion.

Toyota took 1-2 (Bjorn Waldegard and Per Eklund) in 1982. Lancia's Walter Rohrl inherited a lucky win after Michel Mouton's Audi

engine failed just stages from victory. At the third time of asking, however, Audi won in 1984, with Stig Blomqvist.

Over the following years the event became a more regular player in the series and it became a happy hunting ground for many crews. Carlos Sainz took a hat-trick of wins from 1990–1992 before Colin McRae scored his first World Rally win in 1993 and took the following two for good measure. Rotation out of the WRC for 1996 saw Richard Burns win the Asia-Pacific Championship qualifier before Kenneth Eriksson, Sainz again, Tommi Makinen and, last year, Marcus Gronholm brought the story up to date.

Star of the Show

Until Colin McRae won this event in 1993, Britain's only other WRC event winner was Roger Clark in 1976. McRae revelled on the New Zealand roads (most notably over the corkscrew Motu Road stage where none could match his speed) and his three consecutive wins put him and British rallying firmly on the map, culminating in his 1995 World crown.

SAN REMO

If you want slick organisation and a modern outlook, go to Australia. If you want sheer passion for motorsport then you need look no further than San Remo. If it doesn't sweep you along with it, then you need to get out more.

In terms of age, the San Remo Rally is second only to Monte Carlo. Two early events were run in 1928 and 1929, both being won by Major Urdareanu of Romania in a Fiat.

The event then took a major sabbatical and didn't return until 1961, when the de Villa brothers won what was known as the Rally of the Flowers. The name was a reference to the market gardening of the region. To this day, anyone travelling the eye-opening autostrada that links the south of France to Tuscany can't fail to notice the banks of greenhouses that cling to the slopes above San Remo.

Eric Carlsson (co-driven by Gunnar Palm in a Saab 96) was among the early non-Italian winners of the event, as was Jean-Francois Piot

of France in a Renault Gordini. Piot beat Paddy Hopkirk's Mini in the 1967 event although Hopkirk's co-driver, Ron Crellin, admitted some years afterwards that they never should have been accredited with second place. The car broke a driveshaft near the end of the final stage and there was no way that the car would make it back to the finish in San Remo.

A tractor was persuaded to push the car up the hill, after which it could coast down the other side. The plan was to change the driveshaft at service, but by then there was not enough time. The final control was the other side of a tunnel and so one of the BMC service cars, with one last shove, catapulted the Mini and its now terrified crew through the tunnel. With a handbrake turn round a bewildered traffic cop, Hopkirk then coasted into the control to claim his prize.

In 1968 the event called itself the San Remo Rally for the first time and, apart from a couple of years as the San Remo-Sestriere Rally of Italy, the title stuck. It became, however, a rally of two parts with the first and third sections held on the asphalt roads above the town that gives the rally its name and with a middle gravel section several hours of driving down the motorway in Tuscany.

Only recently has that format been changed. While few mourned the passing of that mind-numbing drag from one area to the other, many missed the chance to compete in one of the most beautiful areas of the country. The sight of the cars lined up in parc ferme in front of Pisa's most famous landmark contrasted old and new.

Mastering the challenge of the two areas (the northern section was on asphalt while the

Spectators line the roads hours in advance to get the best viewing spots.

southern stages were on gravel) was an art in itself. Teams would carry out a major suspension swap between the two regions. Also, as the four-wheel drive revolution took hold in the early 1980s, a fascinating game of hare and hounds took place. Lancia's two-wheel drive cars invariably led after the asphalt while Audi, and latterly Peugeot, hit back on gravel. The trick was to be so far ahead after the first asphalt stages that, when the four-wheel drive cars set the pace on gravel, you could be close enough to wrest back the lead once you got back to asphalt.

The proximity of the mountains often left the roads streaming wet with torrential rain on that final night and it needed both bravery and skill to win. In 1981 Michele Mouton proved brave enough to be the first (and only) woman to win a round of the WRC.

Typically this was a rally that attracted controversy. A decade ago Lancia came under widespread scrutiny because of its habit of changing the fire extinguisher bottles that fed into the engine bay at every service point, despite their never having had to be used. Naturally the team denied any suggestion that the bottles contained anything other than fire extinguishant and were certainly not responsible for the cars' unusual turn of speed.

More serious was the 1986 event where early leaders Peugeot were thrown out of the rally after two of the three legs. The Italian scrutineers persuaded the FIA stewards that the French cars were fitted with illegal underbody aerodynamics. The team was refused an appeal and Markku Alen went on to win for Lancia. Second place on that year's RAC Rally and a final win in America gave Alen the World Championship ... for 11 days. The FIA court of appeal agreed that the San Remo affair had been badly handled and annulled the results, handing both back titles to Peugeot.

It has been a happier event since then although team orders and time penalties for illegal recces have turned up from time to time. There's nothing predictable when the Italians are let loose in motorsport!

CORSICA

They sometimes call this the Rally of 10,000 Corners. Corsican roads are seriously twisty and test a driver's stamina like no other. The drops off the edge are not for the faint-hearted either! Its new date has certainly raised its championship profile.

Corsica has transformed its event quite dramatically in recent years and this is very much a step in the right direction. Critics had considered the organisers to be insular in more than just the geographical sense. However, a relatively recent review of the event's organisation has revealed a great improvement in attitude.

Ironically, the latest change to the event is a switch of date from its seemingly traditional early May slot to a new position in mid-October. This could have interesting consequences.

The early Corsican rallies, or Tour de Corse as the events were better known, ran in November. At that time of year the weather is not so pleasant and the Isle de Beaute does not bask in sunshine. Rain, torrential at times

Sunshine and clear, blue waters. It could only be Corsica.

thanks to the meteorological effect of the high mountains, can be a factor even in May so the October slot will be fascinating!

Those early events must have been a nightmare. The Corsican roads are unbelievably twisty and there's probably not a local word for 'straight'. Add the effects of rain, mud and fallen leaves, along with the distinct possibility of snow, and some pretty basic technology at the drivers' disposal, and you had one of the toughest events in the calendar.

While Michele Mouton has gone on record as the first and only woman ever to have won a World Rally Championship event (four times in fact), the first winner of the Tour de Corse was also a woman. In 1956, Gilberte Thirion headed a Renault Dauphine 1-2 to set the ball rolling on this event.

A string of mainly French victories followed as one might expect, with the likes of Renault and Citroen (Rene Trautmann and Lucien Bianchi scored a Citroen 1-2 in 1961) dominating the early results. Porsche and Alfa Romeo won occasionally, but it wasn't until the late 1960s that the big hitters began to feature.

In 1967, Sandro Munari and Pauli Toivonen led a Lancia Fulvia 1-2 ahead of Vic Elford's Porsche, undoubtedly the highest-quality podium in the event's history to that point, although the following year's trio of Jean-Claude Andruet (Alpine Renault), Rauno Aaltonen (Lancia) and Bianchi (Alfa Romeo) ran it close.

Sportscar legend Gerard Larousse won with a Porsche 911 in 1969 and the French had clearly established a firm stranglehold on the event. Bernard Darniche (six times), Andruet, Jean-Luc Therier, Jean Ragnotti and current

Getting There

You'll be getting to know Nice airport quite well by now! From there (or Marseilles) you pick up an onward flight to Ajaccio. Alternatively take a ferry from a variety of Mediterranean ports. Corsica has no great hotels and can be expensive.
www.ffsa.org/rallye-de-france

Peugeot team boss Jean-Pierre Nicolas all got their hands on the silverware in the mid-1970s and early-1980s. Only Munari got in their way before Markku Alen scored Finland's first wins in 1983–1984.

In the middle of all this the event changed its format to that more recently associated with the Corsican Rally. The change came in 1979 when the date moved to spring. The organisers also scrapped overnight stages and considerably extended the mileage.

The mid-1980s should have been a boom period for the event. With cars hitting power levels well over 500bhp, the twisting island roads were the ultimate challenge. However, in 1986 and with the sport still reeling from the spectator deaths in Portugal, Corsica provided an even blacker day.

Henri Toivonen was widely expected to win that year's World Championship and was driving like a man possessed in Corsica. Then, with no obvious explanation, neither at the time nor since, his Lancia plunged off the road near Corte and exploded in flames. Toivonen and co-driver Sergio Cresto were killed instantly.

Within weeks the FIA had scrapped the Group B formula (effective at the end of the season) and cancelled its proposed Group S successor. Bruno Saby won the 1986 Corsica Rally, but the champagne remained unopened and the event is remembered only for the tragedy.

Bernard Beguin's victory the following year (in a Prodrive BMW M3) was a rare success for a two-wheel drive car in an era already dominated by four-wheel drive. Didier Auriol proved that asphalt was still open to all-comers

when he took the first of his six wins in 1988 and his Sierra RS Cosworth gave Ford its first WRC win in seven years.

Over the next six years Auriol bagged a further five wins to equal Darniche's record and was never out of the top two places. Carlos Sainz was twice a winner in the 1990s, as was Colin McRae, while the 1999 event contained another controversial win for Philippe Bugalski's Citroen Xsara. It was not registered for the championship, worked to a favourable set of kit-car rules, and its success really upset the championship regulars. But that's another story.

The scenery in the villages is as spectacular as the action on the stages.

Star of the Show

French ace Didier Auriol did not win the world title until 1994, but by then he'd won his 'home' event five times and would add a record-equalling sixth the following year. A hat-trick in 1988–1990 secured his mantle as King of Corsica and with wins for Ford, Lancia and Toyota the 2000 SEAT team leader had also proved pretty versatile.

AUSTRALIA

It is a widely held belief that Rally Australia is the event by which the others are judged, and it's easy to see why. The stages may not be classics, but the Australian organisation and forward thinking are second to none.

Catalunya and, since 2000, Cyprus may be newer events, but Rally Australia always seems fresh each season. The Perth-based rally has only a minor facelift each year but it shows that the team behind the event is not one to sit back and relax for a moment.

It's a crucial aspect of this event, which is currently defending itself against a hostile takeover bid by the city of Melbourne, eager to add Australia's premier rally to its tenure of the Grand Prix. Perth is fighting hard, but many believe that it can only delay the inevitable.

Meanwhile this is an event to be enjoyed. Slick organisation and a firm grasp on commercial reality combine to ensure that there are few gripes when the teams hit town. The event has had to create a spectator demand, for the Aussies are not famously known for their love of motorsport. To that end, while it races off into the nearby forests for three days, the master-stroke has been the creation of the Langley Park superstage in the heart of Perth itself.

Initially Perth hosted a street stage through the restaurant quarter but, while it certainly made folk aware that the rally was in town, not everyone wanted a noisy backdrop to their evening meal. Thus the organisers created the biggest and best superspecial stage in the entire championship and made it a pivotal part of the event. Instead of simply visiting it on the way past, as so many other events do, the cars return there each evening to round off the day's action. By that time the spectators have been able to enjoy all manner of demonstrations and match races and, even after the rally stage is over, heavy-duty pop concerts have extended the party long into the night. In short, the place has a special atmosphere.

The rally was first held out of the yachting city of Fremantle in 1988, with Sweden's Ingvar Carlsson taking the honours for Mazda. It was very much a test event and, having passed successfully, the event joined the championship programme in September the following year.

Early summer in Australia as the rally boys hit town.

Getting There

For many this is the best event of the year. Flights to Perth are cheaper than to New Zealand and there's plenty to enjoy when you get there. Well-organised spectator packages make it simple to follow. Great holiday choice, too!

www.rallyaustralia.com/

The ancient drowned forest around Wellington Dam is a well-known feature at the event.

This has very much been Juha Kankkunen's rally. He won the first WRC qualifying Rally Australia, took the next two events straight off and added the 1993 title for good measure. From 1989–1995 he was never outside the top three.

Experience is crucial on this event and many have arrived expecting a relatively easy run, only to discover that this is one of the most technical events of the year.

The road surface in Western Australia comprises millions of tiny ball-bearing shaped stones (it's actually magnetic bauxite) that make the surface as slippery as wet soap on a marble bathroom floor. Tyres need to be specially moulded with what has become known as the 'Australia' tread pattern. It has large blocks cut out so that the stones bind together and grip much like snow would when turned into a snowball. Without this pattern, drivers would simply skate about helplessly.

The roads are equally tricky. Basically smooth and quite fast, the surface drains well and so there is no need for ditches at the side of the road. This means that the trees (some little more than solid stumps) are a lot closer than on other events and that brings its own hazard.

Tragically this accounted for the event's darkest day, in 1993, when Kiwi ace 'Possum' Bourne hit a stump at high speed. Bourne survived unscathed but, despite the rapid arrival of the rescue helicopter, co-driver Rodger Freeth succumbed to massive internal injures before he could reach hospital.

Position on the road makes a major difference to driver performance and it is a fact that the first five cars act merely as sweepers for the sixth. Colin McRae proved this in 1998, turning sixth place (a minute off the lead) into first after only three stages in the Bunnings forestry complex. Turbo failure cost him the chance to hold that advantage, but he had made the point.

The Aussies love a good party and so there was great delight in 1996, and again in 1999, when Tommi Makinen clinched the World Championship in Perth. Generally speaking it must be said that there would be great support if the FIA should decide to reshuffle the calendar and make this event the season's finale. Since 1997 the event has enjoyed a November date, in early summer sunshine, and few have a great desire to tear themselves away from that for the trek to Britain and a cold, dark and wet end to the season.

Star of the Show

Rally Australia entered the World Rally Championship in 1989 and Juha Kankkunen won the first three events! A fourth win in 1993 secured Toyota's first world crown and Kankkunen's fourth (then a record number of titles). The Finn is the most successful driver of the World Championship, although others are closing on his position at the top of the win list.

GREAT BRITAIN

Round 14: November 22-25

Rain, wind, snow, ice and only a few hours of daylight make Britain's WRC round one of the trickiest. It is in the middle of a transition period and it will be a while before we see what kind of event emerges.

The event formerly known as the RAC Rally sounds like an egotistical pop star, yet the fact remains that for most of Britain's rally fans, the clumsily named Rally of Great Britain will for ever be 'the RAC'.

The name epitomises the identity crisis that faces this long-established event. Once it ran pretty much all over the country, briefly visiting every possible patch of rally country from Scotland to the south west, Yorkshire to west Wales and a whole raft of stately homes in the centre. Now, thanks to the need to keep the event closer to its home base, the event has centred on Wales with the headquarters in the centre of Cardiff. Rally GB? The fans (at their peak rumoured to have been more than two million) certainly don't think so.

This is a rally with a long and often glorious history, but for too long the organisers put their heads in the sand, did barely enough to hang on to their World Championship status and stood shoulder to shoulder with the Monte Carlo organisers for their trenchant attitude to change.

The event began in 1932 as little more than a touring assembly with a few driving tests to see who was best. Rumour has it that Colonel A.H. Loughborough, the supposed first winner (no official results were declared until 1953, the 11th event), let his chauffeur do most of the driving!

Eventually, after abandoning the Monte-style format with several start towns and a common finish on some seaside promenade, the 1959 event settled on Blackpool as a start venue, and this remained for five years until a London base was adopted.

Gradually the event, under the inspired leadership of Jack Kemsley, turned its back on seafront autotests to decide the winner and moved into the forests. The 1959 event included a few special stages, but it was the 1960 rally that finally propelled the event on to the world map.

Until then all the winners had been British, but now the Scandinavians came in force. Erik Carlsson took three in a row (1960–1962) and Tom Trana the next two. Rauno Aaltonen and Bengt Soderstrom added to the visitors' tally before the 1967 event was

Richard Burns plunges into the water splash at Sweet Lamb.

Night action is very much a part of Rally GB thanks to its November slot.

famously cancelled at the 11th hour because of a foot-and-mouth disease outbreak.

The Scandinavian domination continued again and it was 1972 before Roger Clark finally broke the stranglehold, albeit briefly. Clark's 1972 success was the first for Ford since Gerry Burgess won the 1959 rally and it marked an eight-year period of unbroken victories for Ford. Timo Makinen became only the second driver to take a hat-trick of wins (1973–1975) before Clark's 1976 victory, the first WRC win for a British driver and the last until Colin McRae won the 1993 New Zealand Rally.

Hannu Mikkola twice won back-to-back RACs, the first pair for Ford, the other for Audi, but while his four wins remain a record, he was twice denied the chance to join Carlsson and Makinen as a hat-trick winner. Colin McRae might have a tenuous claim to a place alongside the greats, because his three wins were broken only by the year when the event was rotated out of the World Championship and was won by Armin Schwarz's Toyota, with McRae a non-starter.

After Clark's 1976 success the event returned to Scandinavian hands for another 14 years before Carlos Sainz topped the score sheets, although Juha Kankkunen has kept a Finnish hand on the magnificent gold trophy.

The event has had its fair share of drama and controversy, but the most recent memories feature McRae's 1995 victory that also landed him the coveted world title. They must also include the dramatic conclusion to the 1998 event where Richard Burns's first win (of three) on his home event was overshadowed by Sainz's

retirement yards from the end of the final stage. It handed the title to Tommi Makinen, who had retired in bizarre fashion on the opening day after crashing on a patch of oil left by an old Hillman Imp.

For most of the Scandinavian years top British drivers were as rare as a British tennis player in the second round of Wimbledon. Now, with the emergence of McRae and Burns on to the forefront of the world stage, recent Rally GBs have seen homegrown success and the two heroes start each time as favourites for victory. The need to control the traffic jams has further slashed the access points to the forests, but with the chance of a home win now a real possibility, the atmosphere out on the course more than makes up for the bleak conditions.

Star of the Show

Roger Albert Clark was destined to win the (then) RAC Rally. His 1972 victory preceded the World Championship by a year but ended the Scandinavian domination of the event and began an eight-year winning streak for Ford. His 1976 follow-up was the first WRC success by a British driver – a record that stood for 17 years before Colin McRae joined him in 1994.

2000 REVIEW

What a season to kick off the 21st century! Rallying turned on the heat as never before with more manufacturers, more excitement, closer competition and more drama than you could shake a stick at.

At the end of the year Peugeot's returning lion had swept the board with the big prizes, the manufacturers' championship nailed in Australia and the driver's title following it on the final round. Marcus Gronholm has picked up Tommi Makinen's fallen mantle and was the clear winner of the Rookie of the Year. Peugeot began the season in despair with all three cars failing to start their engines for day two of the Monte Carlo Rally, but by the end of the year this was the team that held all the aces. Should the rest be afraid in 2001? They should be very afraid...

Ford got its reliability sorted out while Subaru rose, fell and rose again to ensure that British fans supporting Colin McRae and Richard Burns respectively can have plenty to look forward to this coming season.

The sport proved strong enough to bear the news that SEAT was pulling out at the end of the year without breaking stride. With the huge investment taking place behind the scenes to improve 'the show' as far as television audiences and live spectators alike are concerned, the future looks rosy.

For the next few pages, however, let's look back on what might have been rallying's best season ever.

(Above) Richard Burns took a crushing win on the Safari Rally as Subaru swept the board unopposed. (Below) Snow time at the Swedish Rally.

Defending champion Tommi Makinen leaps into action at the Portuguese Rally, but broken steering would later scupper his chances.

THE YEAR IN PICTURES

Colin McRae spent half an hour trapped in his car after a massive shunt in Corsica. Despite an operation, he returned 11 days later for San Remo.

Easy does it. Marcus Gronholm guides his Peugeot safely around the Rally GB course to secure his first World Championship.

MONTE CARLO

It seemed as though nothing had changed. Tommi Makinen won the Monte Carlo Rally and we all thought that we were in for a repeat performance of 1999. It wasn't to be, but Makinen and Mitsubishi enjoyed winning the season's most prestigious event.

Victory in Monte Carlo was as good as it got for defending champion Tommi Makinen.

Gilles Panizzi and Richard Burns battled it out for the lead over the first three stages of the 2000 series opener, but Tommi Makinen took over the lead on stage four and that was that.

However, while there might not have been much of a battle for the lead to consider, there was plenty going on both on and off the stages.

Carlos Sainz had signed for the Ford team once he knew that his 1999 employer, Toyota, was pulling out and heading for Formula One. With very little time at the wheel of the Focus, the Spaniard was circumspect over the early stages of the race, but 11th place still became fourth at the end of the opening leg. One stage later and he was second, a position he would hold to the finish. Ford might have filled both remaining places on the podium, but fate stepped in to deny Colin McRae third place when his engine exploded on the final stage.

Peugeot warned that its first full season since 1986 was a test session for a full attack in 2001, but the local fans and the media were having none of it. This might have been the Monte Carlo Rally, but it is essentially a French event, as that's where the stages are located.

Peugeot is irrefutably the French rally team and so was expected to win. It was all deeply embarrassing, therefore, when all three cars failed to restart for day two, thanks to problems related to plunging overnight temperatures.

Richard Burns' Subaru suffered a similar fate, leaving Juha Kankkunen to take the third spot thanks to a blistering run over the classic Sisteron stage that kept SEAT's young star Toni Gardemeister at bay in fourth. Gardemeister's team mate, Didier Auriol (another Toyota refugee) suffered engine failure a few stages from home, while Armin Schwarz avenged Skoda's false start on the previous year's event (when both Octavias were out before the first stage), by taking the team's first points of the season.

The event organisers reacted badly when the FIA safety delegate instructed them to cancel a stage due to dangerous spectator numbers. The resulting press release condemning his decision resulted in the Automobile Club of Monaco being hauled before the FIA to explain their actions, and the event stays in the series this year only by the skin of its teeth.

14 stages – 381.31kms

	Driver/co-driver	Team
1	Tommi Makinen /Risto Mannisenmaki	Mitsubishi
2	Carlos Sainz/Luis Moya	Ford
3	Juha Kankkunen/Juha Repo	Subaru
4	Toni Gardemeister/Paavo Lukander	SEAT
5	Bruno Thiry/Stephane Prevot	Toyota
6	Freddy Loix/Sven Smeets	Mitsubishi

Rally leaders: SS1, Panizzi; SS2-3, Burns; SS4-15, Makinen.

Stage Winners: Makinen (SS2, 4, 5, 8, 10, 12); Kankkunen (SS7, 13); C McRae (SS9, 11); Sainz (SS14, 15); Panizzi (SS1); Burns (SS3); SS6 cancelled.

Weather: Cold and sunny with snow and ice on high ground.

SWEDEN

R2, Karlstad, Sweden. Feb 10–13, 2000

The announcement of Peugeot's return made the established teams sit up and take notice. Peugeot bounced back from Monte Carlo, and a crushing victory for Marcus Gronholm in Sweden warned of what lay ahead from the silver dream racers.

Tommi Makinen may have finished only seven seconds adrift of Marcus Gronholm at the end of the Swedish Rally, but Peugeot's lanky Finn described his victory as easy. The Peugeot 206WRC is definitely an easy car to drive and seems to be beautifully balanced. It has hit the ground running and is far more competitive than many of its older rivals.

Gronholm could have stretched his legs a little more if required, but the man who has had so many big breaks, and failed to capitalise on any of them, wasn't about to take any more risks than absolutely necessary.

Six points for Makinen was a disappointment. He'd started the event as a strong favourite, having won three of the previous four Swedish rallies, although, as things turned out later in the year, six points was a worthy haul.

Behind these two Colin McRae just edged out Thomas Radstrom for third on the final stage after the pair had swapped places in the closing miles. For McRae this was like winning the event: he hadn't finished in his previous nine outings. The Focus was proving to be somewhat of a mystery car – one minute it was fast and reliable, the next it could be as fragile as a piece of paper. The fact that team-mate Carlos Sainz retired with engine failure showed that the team wasn't out of the woods just yet.

Radstrom was one of several drivers at the start of the season who would achieve good results with an ex-works Toyota Corolla. Bruno Thiry had taken fifth in Monte Carlo and now Radstrom's fourth place showed that there was still life in the old dog yet.

From the old to the new. Hyundai made its series debut with the Accent WRC and, while

19 stages – 377.89kms	
Driver/co-driver	*Team*
1 Marcus Gronholm/Timo Rautiainen	Peugeot
2 Tommi Makinen/Risto Mannisenmaki	Mitsubishi
3 Colin McRae/Nicky Grist	Ford
4 Thomas Radstrom/Tina Thorner	Toyota
5 Richard Burns/Robert Reid	Subaru
6 Juha Kankkunen/Juha Repo	Subaru

Rally leaders: SS1, Radstrom; SS2–20 Gronholm.

Stage Winners: Gronholm (SS2, 5, 6, 8, 10, 11, 14); Radstrom (SS1, 16, 18, 19); Burns (SS3, 17); Makinen (4, 15); C McRae (SS20); SS7 cancelled.

Weather: Cold and sunny with very little snow.

neither Kenneth Eriksson nor Alister McRae set the world alight, both made it to the finish line first time out.

The pre-event talk had been of the weather. Once this was the only guaranteed snow rally of the year, but now it was more like a gravel event with some snowy stages thrown in. As the circus hit town a couple of days before the event there were some who wondered if the rally could go ahead at all, and the organisers may well have to consider a new base for future events.

Marcus Gronholm scored his first World Rally win in Sweden.

SAFARI

Richard Burns served notice of his intention to win this year's championship with a crushing display, leading virtually from start to finish. Apart from his Subaru team-mate Juha Kankkunen, who finished second, Burns faced little competition.

The absence of a single puncture proved crucial to Richard Burns' Safari win.

Richard Burns started the Safari Rally as strong favourite and he delivered the goods over the Kenyan plains. SEAT's Didier Auriol had recorded the fastest time on the opening section of this classic event (unique in the safety-conscious modern era for allowing flat-out action on roads still in everyday use by ordinary folk), but thereafter it was Burns all the way.

Tracking the Englishman was his Subaru team-mate Juha Kankkunen, but the Finn was almost five minutes – not a lifetime in Safari terms – behind at the finish, with Auriol another 18 minutes adrift in third place.

The talking point was the performance of Subaru's Pirelli tyres and while the Italian manufacturer left Kenya with its head held high, rivals Michelin were left amid a pile of shredded rubber. Neither Subaru had a single puncture and there, in a nutshell, was the story of the event.

Auriol's third place was a superb result for SEAT, marking the first decent finish for the team since the Frenchman's arrival.

Ford had decided not to fit its cars with the familiar 'snorkel' systems to keep air intakes clear of the deep water that is so often a feature on the Safari, and this cost Colin McRae a finish.

Although the weather was dry (Kenya had not seen rain in months), spectators had dammed the rivers to make life more spectacular. McRae had survived a major suspension failure on the first day, but he was going no further when his engine gulped down a lung-full of water. Third place was gone, in another non-finish for the Scot.

Top Ford driver at the finish was Carlos Sainz in fourth, although he had to rely on the team's Norwegian apprentice, Petter Solberg, slowing in the final miles of the event, to let him move up a spot and improve his points haul.

The Peugeots were out of the equation, if not the headlines. Marcus Gronholm's clutch packed up while Gilles Panizzi was already out with broken suspension and later incurred a $50,000 fine for attacking fellow competitor Roberto Sanchez. Mitsubishi also suffered a wipeout, whereas Safari newcomers Skoda got both their Octavias home in the top eight, Armin Schwarz once again bagging points.

Makinen continued to lead the championship after the Safari, but Burns was trailing by only four points. Was this the beginning of the end for Makinen's four-year reign as king?

12 stages - 1060.70kms

	Driver/co-driver	Team
1	Richard Burns/Robert Reid	Subaru
2	Juha Kankkunen/Juha Repo	Subaru
3	Didier Auriol/Denis Giraudet	SEAT
4	Carlos Sainz/Luis Moya	Ford
5	Petter Solberg/Philip Mills	Ford
6	Toshihiro Arai/Roger Freeman	Subaru

Rally leaders: SS1, Auriol; SS2–12, Burns.
Stage Winners: Burns (SS2, 3, 4, 5, 10); Sainz (SS6, 7, 8, 11, 12); Auriol (SS1, 9)..
Weather: Hot, dry and sunny.

PORTUGAL

Subaru's gamble to use the new Impreza WRC2000 paid off handsomely. It may look like the old car, but underneath it is some 90% new and a drive of champion stature was needed before Richard Burns could see off a strong challenge from Marcus Gronholm.

Six-and-a-half seconds doesn't seem like much of a margin of victory, but such was the Richard Burns's domination that it might as well have been six-and-a-half minutes.

Dust hanging in the air reduced visibility to dangerous levels. That, coupled with the handicap of that dust starting life as loose gravel to be swept off the surface by early cars so that later runners got the benefit, ensured that Burns had to take the lead three times before he finally got to keep it.

Once again the performance of Gronholm's Peugeot was a revelation. The Finn had been drafted into the team as a back-stop for its two more regular drivers, but now questions were being asked about his programme for the rest of the year. Second place brought him level with Makinen, four points behind series leader Burns, and while Peugeot bosses were still not ready to admit it, Gronholm was now the team's best chance of lifting the title in its first full year back. He'd fought hard with Burns, capitalising on a better start position, but ultimately lost out as Burns reeled him in, cut the gap to 1.7 seconds going into the final stage, and then blasted clear to seal the win.

Engine failure had sidelined Colin McRae once again, but Carlos Sainz upheld the Ford team's honour with third place to stay in touch with the title chasers. Transmission failure halted both Hyundais, while broken steering scuppered Makinen's chances. The best result for Mitsubishi came through Freddy Loix, whose long-term position in the team was in question.

Harri Rovanpera's fourth place again proved the pace of the retired Toyota Corolla, while young Estonian driver, Markko Martin, took another Corolla to seventh. Unfortunately the event was to be denied a clash of the faces of the future when Petter Solberg's Ford Focus clutch gave up the ghost.

With neither Rovanpera nor Martin registered for manufacturer points, eighth-placed Armin Schwarz scored again for Skoda, edging out SEAT's Toni Gardemeister.

Victory enabled Burns to become the first-ever Englishman to hold the series lead and when he was asked at the finish whether he felt that this marked the end of Tommi Makinen's reign as World Champion, he simply grinned and said: 'I sincerely hope so!'

23 stages – 398.35kms

	Driver/co-driver	Team
1	Richard Burns/Robert Reid	Subaru
2	Marcus Gronholm/Timo Rautiainen	Peugeot
3	Carlos Sainz/Luis Moya	Ford
4	Harri Rovanpera/Risto Pietilainen	Toyota
5	Francois Delecour/Daniel Grataloup	Peugeot
6	Freddy Loix/Sven Smeets	Mitsubishi

Rally leaders: SS1, Gronholm; SS2-3, C McRae; SS4-8, Burns; SS9-16, Gronholm; SS17-18, Burns; SS19-21, Gronholm; SS22-23, Burns.
Stage Winners: Burns (SS3, 4, 6, 7, 12, 13, 14, 16, 17, 21, 22, 23); Gronholm (SS1, 19, 20); Sainz (SS9, 10, 18); C McRae (SS2, 5); Rovanpera (SS8); Delecour (SS11); Solberg (SS15).
Weather: Warm and sunny.

Richard Burns' win with the new Subaru put him on top of the world at Portugal.

CATALUNYA

This one mattered a lot to Ford and Colin McRae. The Scot had gone over a year without a win and Ford's $10 million driver was looking elsewhere. His title bid looked to be in tatters and his morale was at an all-time low. Victory was a major boost to all concerned.

The final few stages would be tense. As the crews headed into the final morning McRae held a 4.3 second lead over Richard Burns with local hero, Carlos Sainz, a further five seconds adrift. Sainz could still snatch the win, but realistically this was a battle of the Brits.

The stage time charts showed just how much these three drivers dominated the event. Tommi Makinen took two fastest times, Marcus Gronholm and Armin Schwarz took one apiece, but the rest were split between the podium trio.

Over the wet opening morning Burns looked uncatchable. Had the weather stayed the same all day then the result might have been different. Instead the weather dried, Burns gambled and was caught on the wrong tyres and McRae reeled him in. They were eight seconds apart overnight with Sainz already a distant 24 seconds off the lead. Day two and Burns hit a transmission problem on the long opener, just as McRae struck form and shot

15 stages - 383.09kms

	Driver/co-driver	Team
1	Colin McRae/Nicky Grist	Ford
2	Richard Burns/Robert Reid	Subaru
3	Carlos Sainz/Luis Moya	Ford
4	Tommi Makinen/Risto Mannisenmaki	Mitsubishi
5	Marcus Gronholm/Timo Rautiainen	Peugeot
6	Gilles Panizzi/Herve Panizzi	Peugeot

Rally leaders: SS1-6, Burns; SS7-15, C McRae.

Stage Winners: C McRae (SS6, 7, 9, 12, 14); Burns (SS1, 2, 4); Sainz (SS3, 10, 11); Makinen (SS8, 13); Schwarz (SS5); Gronholm (SS15).

Weather: Wet at first, then sunny.

into the lead. Statistics show that the top four places would not change, but even those who witnessed the battle couldn't quite believe it!

Makinen was out of contention at the end of day two with a broken brake pipe. It was now a three-way race to the line with less than ten seconds covering them.

A broken clutch on the run out to the first stage cost McRae a road penalty that handed Burns the lead. However, an astonishing job by the mechanics got the Focus back on song and once the clocks were running McRae outpaced Burns to stay ahead. On the next stage Burns closed the gap to just 1.2 seconds while Sainz also homed in on the leaders and was now only 5.5 seconds adrift with two stages to go.

The crowds were hanging off the bridges to see the action as McRae eased clear again with Sainz struggling to hang on. With live television for the climax of the race the tension on and off the stages was remarkable, but there was great joy under the Martini awnings when Burns stopped the clocks on the same time as McRae, confirming the 1–3 result for Ford.

Spanish fans pack the bridges to cheer on their heroes.

ARGENTINA

After having victory snatched from him by his team-mate a year earlier, Richard Burns had some unfinished business in Argentina. This time there was no question about the result and Burns stamped his authority on the event in no uncertain fashion.

Fastest time on all but one stage of the second leg, and a total of 13 stage wins out of 22, underlined Burns's performance in Argentina. Marcus Gronholm grabbed a share of the lead during the event, as did Carlos Sainz until his lead was cut short when he slam-dunked the Ford into a bridge parapet.

There was a minor scare on the final morning when, in thick fog, Burns overshot a junction and clouted a large piece of the lunar landscape. Fortunately, the boulder simply rolled away while Burns drove on.

Gronholm was a minute adrift at the finish, while Makinen's third place was a major boost. He had been embroiled in a battle with fellow Finn, Juha Kankkunen, until the Subaru driver stuffed his Impreza into a tree.

Ford had gone to Argentina on a high after the Catalunya result, but Sainz's accident had halved the official entry and Colin McRae's event came to a shuddering halt when the engine failed. This time the cause was more easily explained as the Scot, like many others, had nose-dived his car into the ground after a bump in the middle of a water crossing. It is believed that the sump guard scooped a stone into the engine, where it lay dormant for a day until it finally got jammed in a vital organ.

Petter Solberg actually rolled coming out of that same water splash, but went on to take his second set of championship points.

Don't mention water to SEAT. There's a lot of it in Argentina, but only one river was needed to see off both Cordobas on the same stage. The double-whammy happened just as the team's motorsport director, Vicente Aguilera, was collecting his bags at Cordoba airport.

There's a lot of water in Argentina, but it couldn't stop Burns.

There was better news for Hyundai as Alister McRae collected the team's first points of the season.

Burns went into the final day only nine seconds ahead of Gronholm, but setting a time 22 seconds faster than anyone else on the opening stage put the issue beyond debate. Burns was now 14 points clear in the title race, enough to stay there until at least New Zealand. He'd need that advantage, too…

21 stages - 391.40kms

	Driver/co-driver	Team
1	Richard Burns/Robert Reid	Subaru
2	Marcus Gronholm/Timo Rautiainen	Peugeot
3	Tommi Makinen/Risto Mannisenmaki	Mitsubishi
4	Juha Kankkunen/Juha Repo	Subaru
5	Freddy Loix/Sven Smeets	Mitsubishi
6	Petter Solberg/Phil Mills	Ford

Rally leaders: SS1–2, Burns; SS3–6, Gronholm; SS7–9, Sainz; SS10–14, Gronholm; SS15–22, Burns.
Stage Winners: Burns (SS1, 2, 4, 10, 12, 13, 14, 15, 16, 17, 18, 19, 22); Gronholm (SS3, 8, 20); Sainz (SS6, 7, 9); C McRae (SS11); Makinen (SS21); SS5 cancelled.
Weather: Wet and sometimes foggy.

ACROPOLIS

R7, Itea, Greece. June 9-11, 2000

Ford was having a strange year. Up in Spain, down more or less everywhere else. And now, on what turned out to be the toughest event of the year, Colin McRae and Carlos Sainz took first and second no fewer than six minutes clear of Juha Kankkunen.

The fragile Focus was rock solid in Greece for a 1-2 finish.

Forget the top three drivers for a moment and have a look at the rest of the points scorers. Toshihiro Arai (a little-known but promising Japanese driver), Armin Schwarz (in a still under-developed Skoda) and Abdullah Bakhashab (a Middle East driver contesting occasional events). Where were the stars? Scattered to the four winds – fallen off, broken down or simply too late to continue.

Up at the front the performance of the Fords was incredible. They barely put a wheel wrong and the rest of the pack could only watch and wonder if they would break down. Catching them was impossible and this time the cars held together to record a stunning 1–2 finish.

The only real challenge came from Richard Burns, but the new Subaru had a fragile suspension that lasted only a stage at a time before it became too difficult to control. In the end a turbo failed on the first stage of the final morning and Burns couldn't restart the engine. That handed a massive lead to the Fords over

Kankkunen and the team told its drivers to take it easy and hold station. However, Sainz closed the gap and then shot past McRae as the day unfolded (bringing back memories of Spain 1995). Frantic orders were issued to make him slow down and, eventually, he stopped to let McRae win.

The Mitsubishis both retired with mysterious hub-shaft failures, the SEATs of Didier Auriol and Toni Gardemeister suffered a lost wheel and steering failure respectively, Marcus Gronholm's turbo packed up, Kenneth Eriksson's Hyundai blew its engine and Alister McRae's sister car went over time limping to service on just three wheels.

When Burns retired it seemed that his series lead had evaporated, but with all the carnage occurring elsewhere he fared rather well and was assured of leading up to the start of the Finnish event in August.

Skoda was delighted with fifth place as it meant that it now had the edge on its VAG stablemate SEAT. Ford, on the other hand, was just over the moon!

19 stages - 390.37kms

	Driver/co-driver	Team
1	Colin McRae/Nicky Grist	Ford
2	Carlos Sainz/Luis Moya	Ford
3	Juha Kankkunen/Juha Repo	Subaru
4	Toshihiro Arai/Roger Freeman	Subaru
5	Armin Schwarz/Manfred Hiemer	Skoda
6	Abdullah Bakhashab/Bobby Willis	Toyota

Rally leaders: SS1-2, Gronholm; SS3-15, C McRae; SS16-18, Sainz; SS19, C McRae.
Stage Winners: Solberg (SS4, 14, 15, 17, 18, 19); C McRae (SS2, 3, 5, 7, 12); Burns (SS6, 8, 10, 11); Sainz (SS9, 13, 16); Gronholm (SS1, 4).
Weather: Hot, dry and sunny.

82   ROUND 7 - ACROPOLIS

NEW ZEALAND

New Zealand is the farthest event from the teams' European bases, but it was there that the 2000 championship came alight. Gronholm's victory, a second-place finish for McRae and a pair of broken Subarus, produced a title fight worthy of the name.

Marcus Gronholm's victory was sealed at the start of the second leg when the surprise early leader, Francois Delecour, retired the sister Peugeot with broken transmission.

This was a rally where road position counted for everything. Series leader Richard Burns was seeded first on the road and had to accept that he was going to suffer while his rivals would get the benefit of cleaner roads. After the first leg Burns was eighth while the lowly Delecour led from Petter Solberg and Gronholm.

Into day two and the roles were reversed. Burns raced up the leader board to become embroiled in a battle for second place with Colin McRae, while Gronholm was already way ahead.

Day two started dry, hence Burns' climb, but he then lost the chance to make second place stick when he was caught in a heavy shower on the wrong tyres. McRae moved into the spot like a bullet and the Gronholm/ McRae/Burns battle would enter the final day.

That last day was a tough one to call. It opened with a 31km stage and a rapid Burns looked to have closed the gap. However, on the next stage both he and his Subaru team-mate, Juha Kankkunen, coasted to a halt at the finish with broken flywheels. That left Burns holding just a four-point lead over Gronholm, and eight over McRae, going into Finland, with Ford's 2–3 putting it just one point behind Subaru in the Manufacturers' title race.

Hyundai's final day was a bitter-sweet affair. Alister McRae chalked up the team's first-ever fastest time on that opening stage, only for his car's transmission to seize on the road section afterwards. Team-mate Kenneth Eriksson took more points for the fledgling squad, this time

24 stages – 373.37kms

	Driver/co-driver	Team
1	Marcus Gronholm/Timo Rautiainen	Peugeot
2	Colin McRae/Nicky Grist	Ford
3	Carlos Sainz/Luis Moya	Ford
4	Petter Solberg/Phil Mills	Ford
5	Kenneth Eriksson/Staffan Parmander	Hyundai
6	'Possum' Bourne/Craig Vincent	Subaru

Rally leaders: SS1–9, Delecour; SS10–24, Gronholm.
Stage Winners: C McRae (SS7, 8, 13, 14, 20, 21, 22, 23); Burns (SS9, 10, 11, 12, 19); Gronholm (SS3, 15, 16, 17); Solberg (SS2, 4, 24); Delecour (SS1, 5, 6); A McRae (SS18).
Weather: Mainly dry, but with some showers.

without the help of non-registered crews.

Mitsubishi withdrew both its cars during the event after a string of unsolveable transmission problems. Freddy Loix was the first to go as the team felt his errant car was dangerous, while failed brakes stuffed Tommi Makinen into a bank and he too opted not to continue. Both SEATs crashed out on the final event for the 'old' Cordoba.

Next up was Finland and that wasn't looking good for anyone without a Finnish passport.

Victory in Kiwi-land for Marcus Gronholm was especially sweet.

FINLAND

R9, Jyvaskyla. August 18-20, 2000

Finland threw the World Rally Championship wide open. While Richard Burns crashed out of a challenging second place, Marcus Gronholm won with Colin McRae second. For the first time since Portugal Burns wasn't the series leader and the questions were being asked.

The pressure on Marcus Gronholm was intense yet he led the rally from start to finish. He had been reluctant to discuss the possibility of the title at any point in the season but, at the finish, even Gronholm had to admit that it was now a possibility.

Over the opening day the event quickly developed into a two-horse race, with Burns the only driver capable of living with the Peugeot. Rarely more than a handful of seconds apart, the two rivals were flying. However, on the first stage of the second day, Burns flew just a little too fast into the final corner. He crossed the finish line and recorded a time but the Subaru was in the middle of a series of rolls from which it would not recover. Burns crawled from the wrecked car with a stiff neck and the knowledge that unless something befell Gronholm over the next two days his championship lead was gone.

Nothing did befall Gronholm. With over a minute in hand he was able to cruise, while the battle for second raged behind him. Only a mistake on the final day robbed former SEAT

Pressure? What pressure? A home win for Gronholm.

driver Harri Rovanpera, competing in a private Toyota, of second, the ensuing time penalty enough to drop him behind McRae at the finish.

Fourth place for Tommi Makinen wasn't a bad result in 2000, but for the five-time winner of this event it was considered a disaster. The revised Mitsubishi wasn't working as it should and from his comments to some of the media it seemed that only a watertight contract was stopping him taking up Peugeot's offer for 2001.

SEAT debuted its third evolution Cordoba, but it proved a difficult event. Toni Gardemeister's example coasted to a halt on the run out to the first stage of the second day with no fuel getting to the engine and some frightening handling left Didier Auriol in a distant eleventh. Was Gronholm now the favourite for the title?

23 stages – 410.18kms

	Driver/co-driver	Team
1	Marcus Gronholm/Timo Rautiainen	Peugeot
2	Colin McRae/Nicky Grist	Ford
3	Harri Rovaanpera/Risto Pietilainen	Toyota
4	Tommi Makinen/Risto Mannisenmaki	Mitsubishi
5	Sebastian Lindholm/Jukka Aho	Peugeot
6	Francois Delecour/Daniel Grataloup	Peugeot

Rally leaders: SS1-23, Gronholm

Stage Winners: Gronholm (SS1-2-3-4-5-11-16-17-18-21); McRae (SS14-19-0-3); Burns (SS6-7-9-10*); Kankkunen (SS13-15-22); Makinen (SS10*); Lindholm (SS12). * denotes shared time

Weather: Hot, dry and sunny.

CYPRUS

Carlos Sainz had been out of the winners' circle for over two seasons when he went to Cyprus. When he left he had joined Juha Kankkunen on 23 wins, was back in the title hunt and was a much-rejuvenated Spaniard. A start-to-finish win was the ideal way to bounce back.

When Cyprus was added to the championship as a replacement for China, Sainz and co-driver Luis Moya were quick to criticise. A crushing all-the-way win, however, probably meant that the Spanish duo are much happier about Cyprus right now.

Sainz had rarely been as fired up as this. Throughout the critical opening day, where drivers needed to find the right rhythm, he was beaten only twice (both times by Richard Burns). If the Ford held together then Sainz was heading right back into a title race – a race that was thrown open by the early retirement (through electrical failure) of series leader Marcus Gronholm.

The first day also claimed both Skodas and Didier Auriol's SEAT. When Auriol's team-mate Toni Gardemeister crashed on the following day it completed a miserable week for SEAT, following the pre-rally news of its end-of-season retirement from the series.

By contrast Mitsubishi was bouncing back. Tommi Makinen seemed more relaxed than for a long time while Freddy Loix set two fastest stage times (his first of the year).

Subaru's 2001 signing, Markko Martin, showed why he is part of Subaru's fresh new look by taking sixth place with his private Toyota, ahead of 2001 team-mate, Juha Kankkunen.

Ford moved further ahead of Subaru in the Manufacturers' championship with its second 1-2 of the season. Colin McRae's co-driver, Nicky Grist, said at the finish that it was now not a matter of 'if' but of 'when' Ford clinched the series. He hoped that it would be sooner so that McRae and Sainz could then be freed to fight for the drivers' crown without the

constraint of team orders.

Orders had been imposed in Cyprus, but only a 'hold station' instruction once Sainz and McRae had established their position on the final morning. Francois Delecour had settled into third, while a string of technical maladies forced Burns to accept fourth. From a flying start Subaru was now struggling, although the final four events still favoured a McRae v Burns showdown in the title race.

23 stages – 348.41kms

	Driver/co-driver	Team
1	Carlos Sainz/Luis Moya	Peugeot
2	Colin McRae/Nicky Grist	Ford
3	Francois Delecour/Daniel Grataloup	Peugeot
4	Richard Burns/Robert Reid	Subaru
5	Tommi Makinen/Risto Mannisenmaki	Mitsubishi
6	Markko Martin/Michael Park	Toyota

Rally leaders: SS1-23, Sainz

Stage Winners: Sainz (SS1-3-4-6-7-8-9-17); Burns (SS2-5-15-19-20-22-23); Makinen (SS11-16-18-21); Loix (SS10-13); Kankkunen (SS12); McRae (SS14).

Weather: Hot, dry and sunny.

It was two years since Carlos Sainz last won a World Championship Rally.

CORSICA

Gilles Panizzi won his first World Championship rally, Peugeot took a crucial 1-2 and maximum points in the chase for the Manufacturers title and four drivers now headed the championship with just five points covering them. It should have been a cause for celebration, but Corsica was not that simple.

Gilles Panizzi's win for Peugeot should have been a cause for celebration.

The repercussions from Corsica 2000 could run for some time. The attitude of the locals gave the impression that this was not a welcome event, spoiling the gentle running down of the island after the holiday season and the event organisation left plenty to be desired.

The WRC flirted with tragedy and barely escaped the experience. Any one of three major accidents could have resulted in fatalities, in or out of the car, and left the leading crews begging the FIA to raise its game on the safety front. Tommi Makinen and Freddy Loix both walked away unhurt from major shunts (Makinen's accident put a photographer in hospital with a fractured pelvis) and, worse still, Colin McRae spent a terrifying half hour trapped in the fuel-soaked wreck of his inverted Ford Focus before he could be freed and sent to hospital to begin treatment on a fractured cheek bone and bruised lung. It would be a race against time to be fit for San Remo.

The shame of it is that the accidents overshadowed a spectacular contest. Peugeot issued team orders to halt its two front-running drivers before they risked the team's first asphalt victory, a year after the 206WRC made its debut in Corsica. With Gilles Panizzi leading Francois Delecour by just 0.9 seconds at the time, Delecour was furious, but calmed down quickly after team boss, Jean-Pierre Nicolas, whispered something in his ear.

Marcus Gronholm's fifth place was remarkable as this was his Corsica debut, but the two points kept the Peugeot driver at the head of the drivers' table and with growing confidence that this could be his year. Gronholm ended the event two points clear of Richard Burns (who struggled in Corsica), a further two from McRae and one more from Carlos Sainz. Tommi Makinen was still in the hunt, but it would take a spectacular performance in San Remo to keep him there.

17 stages - 348.41kms

	Driver/co-driver	Team
1	Gilles Panizzi/Herve Panizzi	Peugeot
2	Francois Delecour/Daniel Grataloup	Peugeot
3	Carlos Sainz/Luis Moya	Ford
4	Richard Burns/Robert Reid	Subura
5	Marcus Gronholm/Timo Rautianinen	Peugeot
6	Piero Liatti/Carlo Cassino	Ford

Rally leaders: SS1, Burns; SS2-5, Delecour; SS6-11, Panizzi; SS12, Delecour; SS13-14, Panizzi; SS15-16, Delacour; SS17-18, Panizzi.

Stage Winners: Panizzi (SS2-4-5-6-7-9-10-13); Delecour (SS3-11-12-14); Burns (SS1-15-16); Gronholm (SS17); Sainz (SS18); SS8 cancelled

Weather: Warm, mainly sunny, but with some heavy showers.

SAN REMO

It's hard to know whether the biggest story was Colin McRae's return just 11 days after a cheek rebuilding operation, or the allegations of illegal recceing that almost resulted in a punch-up between the Peugeot drivers?

A year ago the FIA promised to clamp down on drivers who drove rally stages outside of the permitted practice hours and, privately, made a specific target of San Remo. Drivers who needed to visit relatives, or even a popular restaurant above San Remo, needed written permission to do so.

How ironic then that, on the way to said restaurant, several people claimed to have seen Gilles Panizzi, but none were event officials. Team-mate Francois Delecour had 'evidence' of Panizzi's crime in the shape of already used pace note books for the new stages on the day the official recce began. Two stages into the event his fuse blew and he had to be restrained from punching his rival before being led away in tears.

Panizzi predictably denied everything, but set his best times on stages where the rest were cautious. Richard Burns was fastest on the opening stage but from then on it was Panizzi all the way with Delecour trailing behind.

Burns mounted the only serious challenge to Peugeot's domination, but smacked a wall on the second day and by the time he reached service the engine was beyond redemption.

McRae said that the one point he got for finishing sixth was the hardest he'd ever won. Still not fully fit after his Corsica crash, McRae battled to finish just behind his teammate. Tommi Makinen also drove brilliantly to take third and keep his fading title hopes alive for at least one more event while fourth for Marcus Gronholm took him a convincing five points clear.

The jury is still out on the revised 'race track' format for this event that saw stages being run in each direction during the day. The days proved long and drawn out and both stages of the final

16 stages – 344.98kms		
Driver/co-driver		*Team*
1 Gilles Panizzi/Herve Panizzi		Peugeot
2 Francois Delecour/Daniel Grataloup		Peugeot
3 Tommi Makinen/Risto Mannisenmaki		Mitsubishi
4 Marcus Gronholm/Timo Rautiainen		Peugeot
5 Carlos Sainz/Luis Moya		Ford
6 Colin McRae/Nicky Grist		Ford

Rally leaders: SS1, Burns; SS2–17 Panizzi; SS12.

Stage winners: Panizzi (SS2-4-5-7-8-9); Delecour (SS3-5-6-17); Makinen (SS10-13-16); Jean-Joseph (SS11-12); Burns (SS1); Gronholm (SS14); SS15 cancelled.

Weather: Warm and sunny, but with damp morning roads under trees.

day were cut short because of problems after just a handful of cars had started.

San Remo produced plenty of drama, though, to send the series off to Australia in a mood of anticipation. Gronholm and Peugeot could clinch the titles down under, but Burns knew that Oz and the Rally GB would be his strongest events and he promised to win them both...

Another Panizzi win and yet more controversy in the Peugeot camp.

AUSTRALIA

R13, Perth. November 9-12, 2000

Without question this was the most bizarre event ever seen in Rally Australia's 13-year history. The desire not to run first on the road on the region's ball bearing gravel roads led to three days of cat-and-mouse tactics and, in a final twist, the rally winner was then excluded the day after the finish.

A year ago the organisers tried a revolutionary idea, letting crews choose their starting order. The overnight leader got to pick first, second placed man went next and so on. There were some minor faults with the system, but overall it worked well and the drivers loved it. Unfortunately the FIA wouldn't support it for 2000 so back came the tactical shuffling and, with it, farce.

Drivers would blast through the forests and then slow on the final stages to sacrifice their lead and let others do the sweeping for the next day. Once one started they all had to follow suit, but it backfired on Carlos Sainz who stopped too close to the finish line and got himself excluded.

Only on the final day could the drivers really go for it. Even then there was a twist as, six hours after close of play the previous night it was noticed that Makinen had jumped the start of a stage. That brought a ten-second penalty

Peugeot's inherited win put the team beyond reach for the manufacturer's title.

21 stages - 391.17kms		
	Driver/co-driver	*Team*
1	Marcus Gronholm/Timo Rautianinen	Peugeot
2	Richard Burns/Robert Reid	Subura
3	Francois Delecour/Daniel Grataloup	Peugeot
4	Kenneth Eriksson/Staffan Parmander	Hyundai
5	Tapio Laukkanen/Kaj Lindstrom	Ford
6	Toni Gardemeister/Paavo Lukander	SEAT

Rally leaders: SS1-8, Gronholm; SS9-10, Kankkunen; SS11-15, Burns; SS16-21, Makinen (excluded after the event)

Stage winners: Makinen (SS5-8-10*-12-18-19); Gronholm (SS1-2-14-15-20-21); Burns (SS9-11-13-17); Solberg (SS4-6); Delecour (SS7-10*); Kankkunen (SS3); Eriksson (SS16). * shared time

Weather: Warm and sunny.

and dropped him to third on the road. The Finn's 'deliberate mistake' was a smart ploy, and to balance his instant advantage, Burns then stopped to change a wheel before the first stage of the final day and slid back behind Makinen again. Confused? Everyone else was!

And so Makinen stormed on to win while Burns tried in vain to catch Gronholm. Then Makinen was kicked out the following day because of an illegal turbocharger…

In the reshuffled results Kenneth Eriksson bagged Hyundai's best result of the season and Toni Gardemeister scored a rare point for the troubled SEAT squad.

The biggest effect was that Peugeot won the Manufacturers' title while Burns would now have to win Rally GB with Gronholm finishing sixth or lower if Peugeot wasn't to sweep the board. Sainz, McRae and Makinen were now out of the title race and even if it bagged a 1-2 on the final round Ford would lose out to Peugeot on a tie break for the makes title.

GREAT BRITAIN

Richard Burns won the final round with as good a display of driving as you'll ever see, but, in many ways, it remained a hollow victory. He won the battle but lost the war and a hat-trick of Rally GB wins was little more than a consolation prize after Marcus Gronholm took the World Championship.

Burns came to his home event with one clear mission. He had to win the event if he was to have any chance of winning the title. Tommi Makinen's exclusion in Australia turned Marcus Gronholm's five-point lead into a nine pointer and that made Burns' task near impossible. As it turned out, even a five-point deficit would prove to be too much for Burns to overcome.

Burns hit a log pile on the opening stage in treacherous conditions. The Subaru's rear suspension was damaged. He reached service after three stages in 21st place and lucky to be still in the event. However it served only to fire up the Englishman and with crowd support at its highest level, he was urged onwards.

However, while Burns homed in on rally leader Colin McRae in the head-to-head battle the British fans craved, Gronholm's presence between the two was the biggest problem. Burns knew that what happened to his title rival was out of his hands.

McRae threw Burns a lifeline when he rolled out of the event and two stages later Burns was past Gronholm and racing clear. However, the Finn knew he need not get involved in a battle for the event win and from that moment on he backed off as much as he dare.

Burns and Gronholm were the feature race, everyone else merely the supporting event. Carlos Sainz and Tommi Makinen had a scrap for third that eventually went the Finn's way. SEAT finally got some degree of performance out of the Cordoba E3 on its swansong event before the team walked away from the championship. And in a bizarre twist, Skoda and Hyundai ended the series scouring the tie-break

rules to see which had come last in the manufacturers' championship, only to discover that as neither had entered all 14 rounds they weren't going to be classified anyway!

By Sunday afternoon Burns was romping home to only the third hat-trick in the event's history. Taking his place alongside rally legends Erik Carlsson and Timo Makinen was some consolation but he was trying hard to put on a brave face.

Gronholm was ecstatic. At the start of the season he hadn't a WRC win to his name, nor a full programme for the year. By one third distance he'd driven his way into the hearts and minds of Peugeot's hierarchy and to their enormous credit they rethought the game plan. Gronholm got the support and he delivered the title.

Richard Burns may have won the battle, but second place for Gronholm secured the war.

17 stages – 380.80kms

	Driver/co-driver	Team
1	Richard Burns/Robert Reid	Subaru
2	Marcus Gronholm/Timo Rautiainen	Peugeot
3	Tommi Makinen/Risto Mannisenmaki	Mitsubishi
4	Carlos Sainz/Luis Moya	Ford
5	Juha Kankkunen/Juha Repo	Subaru
6	Francois Delecour/Daniel Grataloup	Peugeot

Rally leaders: SS1, Kankkunen & Tuohino; SS2, Solberg; SS3-4, McRae; SS5-6, Gronholm; SS7-11, McRae; SS12, Gronholm; SS13-17, Burns

Stage winners: Burns (SS6-9-12-13-15); McRae (SS7-8-10-11); Gronholm (SS3-4-5); Makinen (SS16-17); Kankkunen & Tuohino (SS1) * shared time

Weather: Wet.

RALLY RECORDS

2000 WORLD RALLY CHAMPIONSHIP FOR DRIVERS

DRIVER	MC	S	EAK	P	E	RA	GR
Gronholm (FIN)	R/0	**1/10**	R/0	2/6	5/2	2/6	R/0
Burns (GB)	R/0	5/2	**1/10**	**1/10**	2/6	**1/10**	R/0
Sainz (E)	2/6	R/0	4/3	3/4	3/4	R/0	2/6
C McRae (GB)	R/0	3/4	R/0	R/0	**1/10**	R/0	**1/10**
Makinen (FIN)	**1/10**	2/6	R/0	R/0	4/3	3/4	R/0
Delecour (F)	R/0	7/0	NS	5/2	8/0	13/0	9/0
Panizzi (F)	R/0	NS	R/0	NS	6/1	NS	NS
Kankkunen (FIN)	3/4	6/1	2/6	R/0	R/0	4/3	3/4
Rovanpera (FIN)	NS	12/0	NS	4/3	NS	NS	NS
Solberg (N)	NS	NS	5/2	R/0	NS	6/1	R/0
Eriksson (S)	NS	13/0	NS	R/0	23/0	8/0	R/0
Auriol (F)	R/0	10/0	3/4	10/0	13/0	R/0	R/0
Arai (J)	NS	NS	6/1	NS	16/0	NS	4/3
Loix (B)	6/1	8/0	R/0	6/1	7/0	5/2	R/0
Gardemeister (FIN)	4/3	R/0	R/0	9/0	R/0	R/0	R/0
Radstrom (S)	NS	4/3	NS	R/0	NS	NS	NS
Lindholm (FIN)	NS	NS	NS	NS	NS	NS	NS
Schwarz (D)	7/0	NS	7/0	8/0	11/0	NS	5/2
Thiry (B)	5/2	NS	NS	NS	NS	NS	NS
Laukkanen (FIN)	NS	NS	NS	NS	NS	NS	NS
Bakhashab (SA)	NS	27/0	NS	R/0	15/0	NS	6/1
Bourne (NZ)	NS	NS	NS	NS	NS	NS	NS
Martin (EE)	NS	9/0	NS	7/0	10/0	NS	R/0

Key: Result/Points; R = retired; X = excluded; NS = Non starter; Bold indicates rally winner

Points scored 10-6-4-3-2-1

2000 WORLD RALLY CHAMPIONSHIP FOR MANUFACTURERS

Manufacturer	MC	S	EAK	P	E	RA	GR
Peugeot	0	**11**	0	9	3	6	2
Ford	6	4	3	4	**14**	0	**16**
Subaru	4	5	**16**	10	6	**13**	4
Mitsubishi	**12**	6	0	2	3	6	0
SEAT	3	0	4	0	0	0	0
Hyundai	NS	0	NS	0	0	1	0
Skoda	1	NS	3	1	0	0	3

Hyundai finished ahead of Skoda on tie-break. Bold indicates rally winner

Points scored 10-6-4-3-2-1 with each team nominating two scoring drivers prior to each event

Rally key:
MC: Monte Carlo **S:** Sweden **EAK:** Safari **P:** Portugal **E:** Catalunya **RA:** Argentina **GR:** Acropolis
NZ: New Zealand **FIN:** Finland **CY:** Cyprus **F:** Corsica **I:** San Remo **AUS:** Australia **GB:** Great Britain

NZ	FIN	CY	F	I	AUS	GB	Pts
1/10	1/10	R/O	5/2	4/3	1/10	2/6	65
R/O	R/O	4/3	4/3	R/O	2/6	1/10	60
3/4	14/0	1/10	3/4	5/2	X/0	4/3	46
2/6	2/6	2/6	R/O	6/1	R/O	R/O	43
R/O	4/3	5/2	R/O	3/4	X/0	3/4	36
R/O	6/1	3/4	2/6	2/6	3/4	6/1	24
NS	NS	NS	1/10	1/10	R/O	8/0	21
R/O	8/0	7/0	NS	NS	R/O	5/2	20
NS	3/4	NS	NS	NS	NS	10/0	7
4/3	R/O	NS	R/O	9/0	R/O	R/O	6
5/2	15/0	NS	R/O	45/0	4/3	R/O	5
R/O	11/0	R/O	8/0	17/0	8/0	9/0	4
R/O	NS	9/0	NS	NS	13/0	R/O	4
R/O	R/O	8/0	R/O	8/0	R/O	R/O	4
R/O	R/O	R/O	11/0	R/O	6/1	12/0	4
NS	NS	NS	NS	NS	NS	NS	3
NS	5/2	NS	NS	NS	NS	NS	2
NS	NS	R/O	NS	12/0	NS	13/0	2
NS	NS	NS	NS	NS	NS	NS	2
NS	R/O	NS	NS	NS	5/2	R/O	2
NS	28/0	R/O	NS	44/0	NS	NS	1
6/1	NS	NS	NS	NS	7/0	NS	1
NS	10/0	6/1	NS	R/O	R/O	7/0	1

NZ	FIN	CY	F	I	AUS	GB	Pts
10	13	4	16	16	14	7	111
10	6	16	4	5	0	3	91
0	2	4	5	1	6	12	88
0	4	2	0	4	0	4	41
0	0	0	1	0	3	0	11
3	1	NS	0	0	3	0	8
NS	NS	0	NS	0	NS	0	8

Marcus Gronholm (right) and Timo Rautianen celebrate victory in New Zealand on their way to the 2000 World Championship.

WORLD RALLY CHAMPIONSHIP FOR DRIVERS
(Inaugurated 1979)

Year	Driver	Nat	Driving
1979	Bjorn Waldegard	S	Ford/Mercedes
1980	Walter Rohrl	D	Fiat
1981	Ari Vatanen	FIN	Ford
1982	Walter Rohrl	D	Opel
1983	Hannu Mikkola	FIN	Audi
1984	Stig Blomqvist	S	Audi
1985	Timo Salonen	FIN	Peugeot
1986	Juha Kankkunen	FIN	Peugeot
1987	Juha Kankkunen	FIN	Lancia
1988	Miki Biasion	I	Lancia
1989	Miki Biasion	I	Lancia
1990	Carlos Sainz	E	Toyota
1991	Juha Kankkunen	FIN	Lancia
1992	Carlos Sainz	E	Toyota
1993	Juha Kankkunen	FIN	Toyota
1994	Didier Auriol	F	Toyota
1995	Colin McRae	GB	Subaru
1996	Tommi Makinen	FIN	Mitsubishi
1997	Tommi Makinen	FIN	Mitsubishi
1998	Tommi Makinen	FIN	Mitsubishi
1999	Tommi Makinen	FIN	Mitsubishi
2000	Marcus Gronholm	FIN	Peugeot

WORLD RALLY CHAMPIONSHIP FOR MANUFACTURERS
(Inaugurated 1973)

Year	Manufacturer	Year	Manufacturer
1973	Renault-Alpine	1987	Lancia
1974	Lancia	1988	Lancia
1975	Lancia	1989	Lancia
1976	Lancia	1990	Lancia
1977	Fiat	1991	Lancia
1978	Fiat	1992	Lancia
1979	Ford	1993	Toyota
1980	Fiat	1994	Toyota
1981	Talbot	1995	Subaru
1982	Audi	1996	Subaru
1983	Lancia	1997	Subaru
1984	Audi	1998	Mitsubishi
1985	Peugeot	1999	Toyota
1986	Peugeot	2000	Peugeot

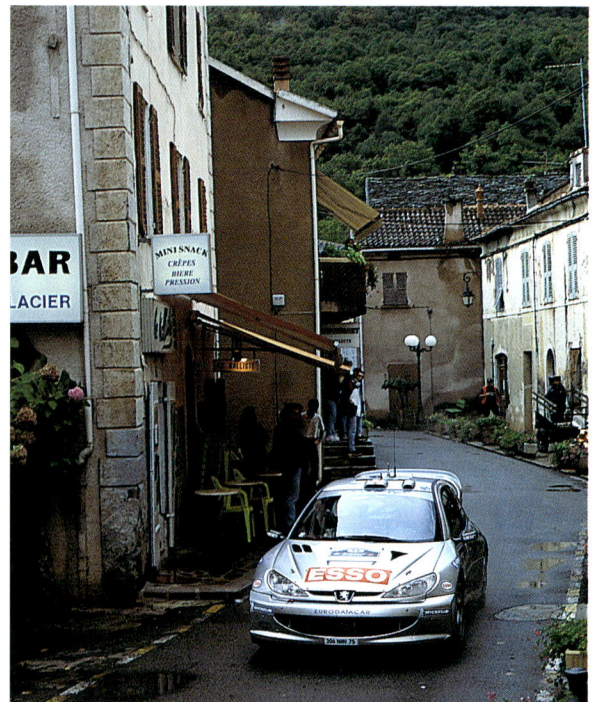

Peugeot swept the board in 2000 taking both the manufacturer's and driver's crowns.

WINNING DRIVERS

23	Juha Kankkunen (FIN)		Gilles Panizzi (F)
	Carlos Sainz (E)		Bruno Saby (F)
20	Markku Alen (FIN)		Kenjiro Shinozuka (J)
	Tommi Makinen (FIN)		Joginder Singh (EAK)
	Colin McRae (GB)		Achim Warmbold (D)
19	Didier Auriol (F)	1	Andrea Aghini (I)
18	Hannu Mikkola (FIN)		Pentti Airikkala (FIN)
17	Miki Biasion (I)		Alain Ambrosino (F)
16	Bjorn Waldegard (S)		Ove Andersson (S)
14	Walter Rohrl (D)		Fulvio Bachelli (I)
11	Stig Blomqvist (S)		Bernard Beguin (F)
	Timo Salonen (FIN)		Walter Boyce (CDN)
10	Ari Vatanen (FIN)		Roger Clark (GB)
9	Richard Burns (GB)		Franco Cunico (I)
7	Bernard Darniche (F)		Ian Duncan (EAK)
	Sandro Munari (I)		Per Eklund (S)
6	Kenneth Eriksson (S)		Guy Frequelin (F)
5	Shekhar Mehta (EAK)		Sepp Haider (A)
	Jean-Pierre Nicolas (F)		Kyosti Hamalainen (FIN)
	Jean-Luc Therier (F)		Harry Kallstrom (S)
4	Francois Delecour (F)		Anders Kullang (S)
	Marcus Gronholm (FIN)		Piero Liatti (I)
	Timo Makinen (FIN)		Joaquim Moutinho (P)
	Michele Mouton (F)		Alain Oreille (F)
3	Jean-Claude Andruet (F)		Rafaelle Pinto (P)
	Jean Ragnotti (F)		Jorge Recalde (RA)
	Henri Toivonen (FIN)		Armin Schwarz (D)
2	Philippe Bugalski (F)		Patrick Tauziac (F)
	Ingvar Carlsson (S)		Tony Fassina (I)
	Mikael Ericsson (S)		Franz Wittmann (A)
	Mats Jonsson (S)		

2000 saw Carlos Sainz get back to winning ways as he climbed to the top of both the winner's rostrum and the driver's standings.

LEADING WINNING CO-DRIVERS

23	Luis Moya (E)
20	Seppo Harjanne (FIN)
	Ilkka Kivimaki (FIN)
18	Arne Hertz (S)
16	Nicky Grist (GB)
	Bernard Occelli (F)
	Tiziano Siviero (I)
14	Juha Piironen (FIN)
13	Christian Geistdorfer (D)
	Hans Thorszelius (S)
10	Bjorn Cederberg (S)
	Risto Mannisenmaki (FIN)
8	Robert Reid (GB)
	Derek Ringer (GB)

He plays hard but he works hard, too. Luis Moya is the world's best co-driver.

WINNING MANUFACTURERS

74	Lancia		Renault
43	Toyota		Renault-Alpine
37	Ford	4	Saab
32	Subaru	3	Mazda
31	Mitsubishi	2	BMW
27	Peugeot		Citroen
24	Audi		Mercedes
21	Fiat		Porsche
9	Nissan (also Datsun)		Talbot
6	Opel	1	Volkswagen

Lancia has been rally's most successful team (with 74 rally wins) and is sorely missed.

WINNING COUNTRIES

115	Finland
64	France
43	Sweden
30	Italy
	Great Britain
23	Spain
17	Germany
8	Kenya
2	Austria
	Japan
1	Argentina
	Canada
	Portugal

MOST WINS IN ONE SEASON

6	Didier Auriol (1992)
5	Miki Biasion (1988, 1989)
	Stig Blomqvist (1984)
	Juha Kankkunen (1991, 1993)
	Tommi Makinen (1996, 1998)
	Colin McRae (1997)
	Carlos Sainz (1991)
	Timo Salonen (1985)
4	Richard Burns (2000)
	Marcus Gronholm (2000)
	Carlos Sainz (1990)
	Tommi Makinen (1997, 1994)
	Hannu Mikkola (1979, 1983)
	Walter Rohrl (1980)

PODIUM CLEAN SWEEPS (1-2-3)

15	Lancia (1976 MC, I*; 1983 F*, I; 1987 USA; 1988 P, GR*,RA, I*; 1989 MC, P, GR, RA; 1990 P**; 1991 I)	3	Fiat (1974 P; 1977 I; 1978 F)
		2	Renault Alpine (1973 MC, F)
5	Audi (1983 S*, RA*; 1984 MC, S, RA)		Subaru (1995 E, GB)
4	Ford (1973 GB; 1975 GB; 1978 GB; 1979 NZ*)		Toyota (1986 CI*; 1993 EAK)
		1	Datsun (1981 EAK*)
			Mercedes (1979 CI*)
			Mitsubishi (1976 EAK)

* First four places   ** First five places

Finland 1994 was the start of Tommi Makinen's home rule.

CONSECUTIVE WINS ON SAME RALLY

5	Tommi Makinen	(Finland 1994-1998)
4	Shekhar Mehta	(Safari 1979-1982)
3	Timo Makinen	(Britain 1973-1975)
	Sandro Munari	(Monte Carlo 1975-1977)
	Bernard Darniche	(Corsica 1977-1979)
	Markku Alen	(Finland 1978-1980)
	Walter Rohrl	(Monte Carlo 1982-1984)
	Miki Biasion	(San Remo 1987-1989)
	Miki Biasion	(Portugal 1988-1990)
	Didier Auriol	(Corsica 1988-1990)
	Juha Kankkunen	(Australia 1989-1991)
	Carlos Sainz	(New Zealand 1990-1992)
	Colin McRae	(New Zealand 1993-1995)
	Richard Burns	(Britain 1998-2000)

TOTAL WINS ON SAME RALLY

6	Markku Alen	Finland (1976, 1978-1980, 1987-1988)
	Didier Auriol	Corsica (1988- 1990, 1992, 1994-1995)
5	Stig Blomqvist	Sweden (1973, 1977, 1979, 1982, 1984)
	Shekhar Mehta	Safari (1973, 1979-1982)
	Markku Alen	Portugal (1975, 1977-1978, 1981, 1987)
	Bernard Darniche	Corsica (1975, 1977-1979, 1981)
	Tommi Makinen	Finland (1994-1998)
4	Hannu Mikkola	Finland (1974-1975, 1982-1983)
	Bjorn Waldegard	Safari (1977, 1984, 1986, 1990)
	Hannu Mikkola	Britain (1978-1979, 1981-1982)
	Walter Rohrl	Monte Carlo (1980, 1982-1984)
	Juha Kankkunen	Australia (1989-1991, 1993)
	Carlos Sainz	New Zealand (1990-1992, 1998)

Bjorn Waldegard was the first World Champion and also the oldest winner of a WRC round.

YOUNGEST WINNERS

Markku Alen (FIN)	24	1975 Portugal
Henri Toivonen (FIN)	24	1980 Britain
Colin McRae (GB)	24	1993 New Zealand
Timo Salonen (FIN)	25	1977 Canada
Stig Blomqvist (S)	26	1973 Sweden
Fulvio Bacchelli (I)	26	1977 New Zealand
Juha Kankkunen (FIN)	26	1985 EAK
Jean-Luc Therier (F)	27	1973 Portugal
Shekhar Mehta (EAK)	27	1973 Safari
Walter Boyce (CDN)	27	1973 USA
Richard Burns (GB)	27	1998 Safari
Ari Vatanen (FIN)	28	1980 Acropolis

OLDEST WINNERS

Bjorn Waldegard (S)	46	1990 Safari
Joginder Singh (EAK)	44	1976 Safari
Hannu Mikkola (FIN)	44	1987 Safari
Pentti Airikkala (FIN)	44	1989 Britain
Kenjiro Shinozuka (J)	43	1992 Ivory Coast
Ingvar Carlsson (S)	42	1989 New Zealand
Kenneth Eriksson (S)	41	1997 New Zealand
Didier Auriol (F)	41	1999 China
Juha Kankkunen (FIN)	40	1999 Finland
Bernard Darniche (F)	39	1981 Corsica
Jean Ragnotti (F)	39	1985 Corsica
Bernard Beguin (F)	39	1987 Corsica

WINNING MARGINS

Smallest   Colin McRae (Subaru Impreza WRC98) beat Carlos Sainz (Toyota Corolla WRC) by 2.1 seconds in Portugal 1998, just edging out the 2.4 seconds win by Juha Kankkunen (Subaru Impreza WRC99) over his team mate Richard Burns in Argentina 1999.

Largest   Achim Warmbold (Fiat Abarth 124) beat Egon Culmbacher (Wartburg 353) by 2h47m2s on the 1973 Polish Rally. Maciej Stawowiak (Polski-Fiat 125p) was the third and final finisher, a further 53m15s behind.

Dead heats   Shekhar Mehta (Datsun 240Z) and Harry Kallstrom (Datsun 1800SSS) tied on the 1973 Safari before Mehta was declared the winner. The only other dead heat involved the Toyota Celica TC Turbos of Juha Kankkunen and Bjorn Waldegard on the 1985 Ivory Coast Rally. The tie was decided in Kankkunen's favour.

Pine trees, lakes and a rally car blasting between the two. McKlein's photographic mastery at work.

The Publishers would like to thank McKlein for their kind permission to reproduce the pictures in this book.

The Publishers wish to express their sincere gratitude to Bob McCaffrey, Colin McMaster, and Reinhard Klein at McKlein for the time and assistance they have contributed to this project.

Every effort has been made to acknowledge correctly and contact the source and/copyright holder of each picture, and Carlton Books Limited apologizes for any unintentional errors or omissions which will be corrected in future editions of this book.